THE JOURNEY

A SPIRITUAL ROADMAP FOR MODERN PILGRIMS

PETER KREEFT

Illustrations by
Jerry Tiritilli

InterVarsity Press
Downers Grove, Illinois

InterVarsity Press® is the book-publishing division of InterVarsity Christian Fellowship®, a student movement active on campus at hundreds of universities, colleges and schools of nursing in the United States of America, and a member movement of the International Fellowship of Evangelical Students. For information about local and regional activities, write Public Relations Dept., InterVarsity Christian Fellowship, 6400 Schroeder Rd., P.O. Box 7895, Madison, WI 53707-7895.

Cover illustration: Jerry Tiritilli

ISBN 0-8308-1682-8

Printed in the United States of America ♾

Library of Congress Cataloging-in-Publication Data

Kreeft, Peter.
    The journey: a spiritual roadmap for modern pilgrims/Peter
    Kreeft.
        p.   cm.
    Includes bibliographical references.
    ISBN 0-8308-1682-8 (alk. paper)
    1. Life.   I. Title.
    BD431.K669   1996
    100—dc20   96-36231
                                                                                    CIP

18	17	16	15	14	13	12	11	10	9	8	7	6	5	4	3	2	1
10	09	08	07	06	05	04	03	02	01	00	99	98	97	96			

The thirteen historical characters in this book—Socrates, Epicurus, Protagoras, Diogenes, Gorgias, Democritus, Thrasymachus, Xenophanes, Parmenides, Aristotle, Moses, Joshua and C. S. Lewis—were all men. But I dedicate this book to a woman who was greater than any of these men because she most clearly and perfectly showed us in one sentence the answer to the fundamental question, When life's journey brings us to a fork in the road, what makes a choice the right one?

When God asked her permission (!) to be born from her womb, her answer was "Be it done unto me according to thy word."

Many of the readers of this book may be Protestants, and I am a Catholic. But this is not an attempt to sneak in some Catholic theology. It is an honest dedication of honest admiration and thanks.

The book points to Christ—the only man in history who chose his own mother. Mary pointed to Christ too; her instructions were "Whatever he tells you, do" (see John 2:5).

I pray daily for reunion between our tragically separated sister churches. I believe Mary showed us the single most important principle for reunion in that single sentence. For we know our Lord's will is unity, and therefore we also know that if we love and obey his will with all our hearts, that is what we will find. When all the instrumentalists obey the Conductor's baton, the whole orchestra will play in harmony.

꧁꧁꧁꧁꧁꧁꧁꧁꧁

Preface

The following story is an allegory, like John Bunyan's *Pilgrim's Progress* and C. S. Lewis's *Pilgrim's Regress*. I thought of entitling it *Pilgrim's Egress*, since it is about a pilgrimage to find the meaning of life, and about an egress, or escape, from ten wrong turns on this pilgrimage. But publishers don't like punny titles. I also thought of calling it *Ten Right Turns*, but I knew the L.I.E. (Left-Wing Intellectual Establishment) would label it "right-wing politics" even though it isn't political at all (and if it were, it wouldn't be either left *or* right).

The story is a roadmap for the most important journey you can make. It is about choosing your philosophy of life.

Here are the ten choices, in logical progression:

1. Shall I question? Shall I go on this quest for truth at all?

2. If I question, is there hope of answers, or should I be a skeptic? Is there objective truth?

3. If there is any objective truth, is there objective truth about the meaning of life?

4. If there is an objective truth about the meaning of life, is it that life is meaningless, "vanity of vanities"?

5. If life has real meaning, is it spiritual and not merely

material?

6. If it is spiritual, is it moral? Is there a real right and wrong?

7. If there is a real right and wrong, a real moral meaning, is it a religious meaning? Is there a God?

8. If there is a God, is God immanent (pantheism) or transcendent (deism), everywhere or nowhere?

9. If God is both immanent and transcendent (theism, creationism), are the Jews (who first taught this idea of creation) his prophets, his mouthpiece to the world?

10. If the Jews are God's prophets, is Jesus the Messiah?

Every one of these choices is momentous. As Robert Frost says in "The Road Not Taken," when two roads diverge, the choice can make "all the difference." Julius Caesar faced such a choice in 55 B.C. when he and his troops crossed the Rubicon River in northern Italy to march on Rome and seize the emperor's crown, thus changing Rome (that is, the whole civilized Western world) from a republic to an empire. His choice of a physical road—to go south rather than north—was dictated by his choice of a spiritual road—that is, by his philosophy of life.

Your mind has roads that are just as real as your body's roads. And just as you must choose whenever you come to a fork in your physical road, you must also choose between different mental roads, different philosophies of life.

Different physical roads lead to different physical destinations. You can't get to the Atlantic Ocean by walking west from Chicago. Different mental roads also lead to different destinations, different destinies:

Sow a thought, reap an act;

Sow an act, reap a habit;

Sow a habit, reap a character;

Sow a character, reap a destiny.

Buddha knew this principle well. The very first line of the most popular Buddhist scripture, the *Dhammapada*, is "All that we are is made by our thoughts. It begins where our thoughts begin, it moves where our thoughts move."

Solomon knew it too. He wrote in his Proverbs: "Keep thy heart [mind, spirit] with all diligence; for out of it are the issues of life" (4:23).

The image of life as a road is probably the single most popular image in the world's literature. It is itself a well-worn road. *The Odyssey, The Aeneid, The Divine Comedy, The Lord of the Rings*—all the great epics are true to life by being true to this image.

Quo vadis? Where are you going? That is the question.

READER: But that is a philosophical question.

AUTHOR: Yes, it is. It's *the* philosophical question.

READER: But I don't like philosophical questions.

AUTHOR: And thus you avoid them?

READER: Yes.

AUTHOR: No.

READER: What do you mean, "no"?

AUTHOR: I mean you can't avoid having a philosophy. Yours is a philosophy against philosophy; but that's a philosophy.

READER: No it isn't. Suppose I just refuse to philosophize.

AUTHOR: You can indeed choose that road. But that is a philosophy too: a bad one, one that deceives itself. You can't choose between philosophy and no-philosophy, only between good philosophy and bad philosophy.

READER: So what?

AUTHOR: So then why not come along on this trip?

ONE

THE BEGINNING

To Question or Not to Question, That Is the Question

𐌾𐌿𐌿𐌿𐌿𐌿𐌿𐌿𐌿𐌿

The following journey was an inside-out dream that I had (or that had me).

It was a dream, but it seemed I was its object, not its subject, the dreamed-about, not the dreamer. My earthly life appeared to me through a heavenly mind. Whether this was my own future heavenly mind, or God's mind, or the mind of an angel, or something else, I could not tell. But in my dream it seemed to me that I was *in* that heavenly mind looking down on my earthly life from above, rather than generating heavenly fantasies from below. This "above-below" reversal was physical as well as mental: instead of being flat on my back on a bed gazing upward, I seemed to be floating, or swimming, face down, as on a wave, body-surfing my life, looking through the water at a lobsterlike creature scuttling across the sea floor. (My name, Kreeft, means "lobster" in Dutch, by the way.)

The journey began in my present, which is middle age—just as Dante's journey did:

In the midway of this our mortal life
  I found me in a gloomy wood astray,
Gone from the path direct. . . .
  How first I entered it, I scarce can say.*

Instead of a gloomy wood, I found myself in a gloomy underground cave. It was enormous, yet I felt claustrophobic. Behind me I saw row upon row of people sitting in comfortable chairs, as in a movie theater. They were all intently watching the play of shadows on a wall of the cave.

I immediately recognized the cave as Plato's—the most famous image in the history of philosophy. As soon as I realized where I was, I heard a harsh and ugly voice speaking in a surprisingly winsome way. It came from the ugliest man I had ever seen. His body was short, fat and twisted; his head was oversized, bald and bulbous; his eyes were froggy; and his nose was pug. I instantly recognized my favorite philosopher.

"Socrates!" I cried joyfully. "Is it really you?"

"As really me as that thing I am looking at is really you," he replied with a cryptic twinkle.

Foolishly trying to impress Socrates with my cleverness, I said, "You mean you can't see my soul, my true self, only my body."

"No, I mean only what I say," he replied. "It's a strange

---

* Dante, *The Divine Comedy*, trans. Francis Cary (London: International Publishing/Bibliophile Books, 1988), canto 1.

habit of mine that you will just have to get used to, I'm afraid. I meant only that if the laws of logic have not been suspended, you can be sure of this, at least: that I am I and you are you. Everything seems to have this strangely stubborn habit of being itself, being logically consistent. As for me, I only try to copy that habit. So do you think you can endure the presence of such a strange creature, one who is constantly out of alignment with people whenever they are out of alignment with truth? One who takes the side of truth against humankind rather than the side of humankind against truth?"

"I would love to have you as my companion, Socrates. Are we going to hang around this cave like bats, or will you lead me out?"

"Well, now, that depends on you. If I guide you on this journey, I will only give you maps, and advice, and arguments. It is you who must choose at each fork in the road."

"What road? I see no road."

"That one." He pointed to a dimly discernible path, strewn with rocks, that climbed steeply, perilously close to abysses, and ducked through tiny tunnels that we would clearly have to crawl through.

"And where is the first fork in the road, the first choice I have to make?" I asked dubiously.

"Why, right here of course. Right here at the beginning."

"I don't see it."

"How can you miss it?"

"Please show me."

"No, let's see whether you can find if for yourself. I will not tell you, only teach you; that is, I will only ask you some questions so that you can tell yourself. That's my style, you know. I just can't make speeches. The last long speech I had to make was a disaster. I can still taste that hemlock!"

"I know your method, Socrates. Ask away!"

"Tell me, then, what does one do at the beginning of any journey?"

"I don't know."

"Yes you do. Just remember the logical law of consistency, the law of identity that we spoke of a moment ago. Now what do you do at the beginning?"

"You begin, I suppose." I was beginning to sound petulant.

"Bravo!" Socrates cheered, as if I had just discovered the theory of relativity. "And does this just happen to you, or do you have to *choose* to begin?"

"You have to choose," I said.

"Well, then, there is your first choice: to begin, or not. To travel, or not. To seek a way out of this cave, or not. To get on this road, or not."

"If I seek a way out, can you guarantee me that I will find it?"

"No. But I *can* guarantee that if you do *not* seek it, you will not find it. Is that not enough to move you to seek?"

"I don't know, to be quite honest with you . . ."

"Please do. Please be quite honest with me. Nothing will work unless you are."

"I have doubts . . . All those people sitting here in this cave—it seems confined, but they seem very happy and content."

"Content they surely are. Whether they are happy or not is another question—unless happiness is nothing more than contentment."

"Don't you think it is?"

"What *I* think is not important—or shouldn't be, to you. What do *you* think?"

"I think it is. If you're content, you're happy."

"Have you ever heard of 'contented cows'?"

"Yes."

"Have you ever watched a cow? Have you ever observed how contented cows are?"

"Yes."

"And how discontented humans are?"

"Yes indeed."

"Tell me, do you think you can be happier than any cow?"

"Yes . . ."

"But you are not as *contented* as a cow?"

"No."

"Then it follows that happiness cannot be the same thing as contentment, does it not?"

"I guess it does."

"So which do you seek? Contentment or happiness?"

"Happiness."

"Good. Then we can travel. You see, I cannot lead you out of this cave unless you *choose* to seek the way out. And to do that, you must be discontent, not content. You must disobey the first law of your society's most popular prophets."

"What law? What prophets?"

"Your pop psychologists, whose law is 'Accept yourself as you are.' In other words, be contented, be a cow. If you will not choose to question their authority, you will not question anything, except the shadows on the wall of this cave."

"I see. My first choice, then, is to choose whether to be Socrates dissatisfied or a cow satisfied."

I thought Socrates was getting ready to congratulate me on this wisdom, and I was getting ready to feel satisfied about my dissatisfaction, when suddenly one of the inhabitants of the cave rose from his seat, turned to me and interrupted. I saw that he came not from one of the small chairs but from a tasteful little walled garden in an unusually pleasant corner of the cave.

"Don't let this charlatan seduce you," he said to me. "There is nowhere else to go except this cave. This is all there is. Tales of another world outside the cave are mere myths. There is no proof of those other realms that Socrates will claim to lead you into. Only children believe such fantasies."

Disconcerted, I now began to doubt and wonder what I was to do. Socrates, however, was neither disconcerted nor upset by the man's attack. He even seemed to recognize him as an old friend. "Why, Epicurus! I suspected you would show up. It seems it is time for us to go to war again for another soul."

"Another *self*, Socrates," Epicurus corrected him. "I must keep reminding you that a self is not a soul but a body, the thing you see here before you. But you keep talking to some invisible spirit or ghost—something that frightens children in their dreams." Turning to me, Epicurus said, "Come with me into my garden of delights. Make the most of the only world you have. Eat, drink and be merry."

"He asks you to abort your escape from this prison," interrupted Socrates. "And instead of beginning the journey on the road to freedom, to sit down by the roadside and play with the pretty flowers."

"The choice is between these real flowers and the imaginary ones in some other unreal world," Epicurus said, still focusing on me. "Why give up the only thing you're sure of?"

I was by now quite perplexed and did not know which guide to believe. I wanted to find out more about Epicurus's garden. "What flowers grow in your garden?" I asked him.

"Whatever brings you pleasure," he replied. "Whatever pleases you. Sex and money seem to be the two most popular ones in your time."

I found that it was impossible to lie or hide or dissimulate in this world. "I must admit I am strongly attracted by your offer."

"It would save endless wear and tear on your shoe leather and your skin," he argued. "Look at all those sharp stones on that road."

I turned to Socrates. "Can you prove to me that it is better to travel than to stay?"

"I cannot," he said. "If you do not want to make this wager, I cannot force you."

"So you are asking me, then, to make a blind leap of faith on your authority."

"I am *not*," he replied, indignantly. "I am asking you to *question* all authorities, to do that thing that sounds so easy but proves so strenuous: to think for yourself, to wonder. Philosophy begins in wonder, you know."

"Suppose I choose not to wonder?"

"Then you have chosen not to choose. Remember—you do not have a choice between some philosophy and no philosophy, only between good philosophy and bad philosophy."

I knew in my heart that he was right. And at that point a strange feeling came over me that I had had only once before in my life: when I proposed to my wife. I felt at the same time totally free to choose either way and totally destined to choose one way alone—totally free and totally fated. I turned my back on the cave and Epicurus's garden, placed my right foot on the road and said: "Here I stand. I cannot do otherwise. God help me!"—and felt freer than I had ever felt before.

I set out alone with Socrates to climb the narrow, steep and rocky path. But after a few steps, I hesitated and turned around one more time. The poor prisoners were still there, unmoving, chained to their shadows by their own addiction to comfort and security. There stood Epicurus in his pretty little yuppie garden.

As I looked back, I half feared being turned into a pillar of salt. What happened instead was that I noticed something, from my higher vantage point on the climbing path, that I had not noticed before. Behind Epicurus's flowers was a skull, grinning.

As I went on, I reflected that this first choice of mine was surely going to be only the first of many choices; that it was the most reasonable and obviously right choice I could ever make; and that it was nevertheless perhaps the hardest and most unpopular choice I would ever make. The road was bare; surely this was "the road less traveled." To follow it I had to deny and disobey a god, the god most of my compatriots worshiped more deeply and absolutely than any other, the god of sameness, the religion of egalitarianism. I had to have the crazy, fanatical courage to seek truth instead as my absolute. *Good grief!* I reflected. *My soul is becoming like Socrates.* I hoped my body would not have to do the same.

As we trudged along, I asked, "Socrates, I am very curious about something. I know that was Epicurus, and I know he lived many years after you died. Yet you knew him as an old friend. Are we beyond time? Are we in . . . in . . . Where are we, anyway?"

Socrates' eyes danced. "No, you are not dead, like me. This world is not the world of the dead, but of the living.

It is your world, not mine. I am sent here as—as an outsider, you might say."

"What were you about to say? A ghost? A prophet? An angel? A dream?"

"All four in a way, and none of the four quite in the way you think," he replied. "The only thing you need to know about me now is that I will be your guide, your teacher. And that I will continue to teach in the only way I ever knew: by questioning. You have chosen to tread this way with me."

I was not completely satisfied with this rather mysterious answer, and I decided to try again: "Another thing, Socrates. I thought *I* recognized Epicurus too, though I have never met him. I realized that only after we left him and his face appeared in my memory superimposed on the face of another man. Now I know where I've seen him before. He's a dead ringer for Hugh Hefner, the head of a network of playpens in my world. Was that Epicurus or Hugh?"

I was not surprised to receive another mysterious answer: "You assume it was one or the other. How do you know it was not both?"

"Do you mean reincarnation?"

"No, I would not now call it that. I was a wee bit off in my guesses back then. But not wholly off. I would call it *reindoctrination.*"

"What do you mean by that?"

"Do you remember, in your Bible, Jesus saying that John the Baptist *was* the prophet Elijah come back?"

"Yes."

"But Jews (and Christians) don't believe in reincarnation, do they?"

"No. So what does it mean, this 'reindoctrination'?"

"Not one soul migrating into two different bodies, but

one philosophy migrating into two different souls. As John the Baptist thought and taught and did what Elijah did, Hugh Hefner thinks and teaches and does what Epicurus did. The similar faces were mirrors of the similar souls."

"But they lived thousands of years apart."

"This is a philosophical story that we are in," he explained, "and we will confront opposite philosophies at each fork of your road. These philosophies are bodied forth to your imagination in the form of philosophers both ancient and modern. Time and history do not matter now. The same philosophies, the same alternatives, the same choices that you confront in your world, we ancients had in ours."

Just as they say, I thought: *the more things change, the more they stay the same.*

TWO

THE SKEPTIC

Is It True That There Is No Truth?

🝖🝖🝖🝖🝖🝖🝖🝖🝖🝖

*I*mmediately *after the road left the cave it forked, and thus we* had to stop while I decided which fork to choose. I was pleased at this development, and Socrates asked me why. I replied, "Because I feared the road would be long and hard and boring before anything happened."

"Oh, it *will* be long. And it *may* be hard. But I guarantee you it will *not* be boring."

The scene that greeted me was this. Far down the right fork there seemed to be an opening in the roof, or the ceiling, of the underground system of roads we were on. Sunlight streamed through the hole and onto the road, mixed with dust and fog. Down the left fork of the road, close by, I saw another kind of light emanating from a bright, colorless room of glass and steel, lined with computer screens and keyboards. The room was sparkling clean and spanking new. At the door to this room, beckoning me, stood a man in a white robe like Socrates', but newer, cleaner and evidently more expensive. It seemed thinner, however.

"Is he another friend of yours among the philosophers?" I asked Socrates.

"We are very old friends, we two," he replied. "That is Protagoras the Sophist. Soon you may seem to see him turn into J. G. Fichte, a philosopher much closer to your own time."

"Another 'reindoctrination,' I suppose."

"Yes."

I knew that I had to listen to Protagoras before I could decide for myself whether to take the left road and enter his room, or the right road and continue my quest for the Great Outdoors.

"What do you seek?" Protagoras asked me.

"Truth," I replied.

"You have found it here," he answered.

"Why is it *here*, in a little room with computers?"

"Because truth is subjective, not objective. Each one of us is in a room like this one. Truth is *your* truth. Whatever you believe is true, is true for you. Man is the measure of all things."

I was a bit taken aback by his dogmatic and preachy style, but I had to investigate his philosophy. "So you are inviting me into your room?" I asked suspiciously.

"No," he answered. "Why should I impose *my* truth on you? You have your own room and your own computer screen. You generate your own 'virtual reality' with it."

"Where is my room?" I asked.

"You are in it already. You always were and always will be. You can never escape your self. That's simple logic. Everything you think appears on your personal computer screen, inside the room of your personal consciousness. There's simply no way out. So you may as well stop trying to find one."

I was pleased that he was beginning to sound logical, but depressed by his philosophy. "What about that sunlight down that road to the right, coming through that hole in the roof? Do you say that is only an illusion?"

"No more and no less than this room is an illusion," he replied. "Whatever you see or think is in your consciousness. Otherwise *you* don't see or think it. So truth is within your consciousness—the only truth you can ever know. You have it already. There's no need to travel any further."

Protagoras's sophisticated argument and smooth voice sounded very convincing to me. Yet I felt sad that my journey was over so soon, and foolish that my quest for some "objective truth out there" was such a folly. I was about to turn down the left fork of the road, toward Protagoras, and do and believe whatever he told me, when the harsh voice of Socrates interrupted me. I had quite forgotten about him.

"Shall we think about this choice of roads before choosing?"

"Oh. Of course," I said, startled. "But I thought I had just done that. There seems to be no way to refute his argument."

"You have thought *his* thoughts. But don't you want to think any others?"

"Of course. But what others? What he says seems so self-evidently true that I am compelled to believe it."

"Compelled by what? By logic?"

"Yes, by logic."

"You will take logic for your teacher then? You will follow the logic of the argument wherever it goes?"

"Yes."

"Good. Then let us explore a little more carefully, if you have the patience, just where the argument does lead. Protagoras!" Here Socrates turned and called to his old friend. "Will you debate with me the great issue of subjective truth versus objective truth here in the presence of this pilgrim so that he can see more clearly to make up his own mind and choose his way?"

"I'd rather not, Socrates. I've said what I have to say. Now it's your turn to try to turn his mind around."

"Debate isn't your style, is it, Protagoras?"

"No, Socrates. I prefer to make beautiful and convincing speeches."

"I'm not surprised. If you do not believe in objective truth, debate becomes a mere game, or a personal contest. For me, debate is two truth-seekers exploring which of two roads really reaches the goal. If you do not believe in the goal, I see why you do not believe in the debate over the way to it. Well, then"—here he turned back to me—"you must choose between the right road and the left. Either objective truth exists, or it does not. These are your two choices, are they not?"

"That is so," I said.

"Now how do you understand the meaning of these two philosophies? What do you mean by 'subjective truth' and 'objective truth'?"

"As Protagoras said, subjective truth means something true *for you*."

"Like a pain or a headache, for instance?"

"Yes."

"Or a dream?"

"Yes."

"Or an opinion, a belief? For instance, I may believe this road is over a mile long, and you may believe it is not."

"Yes, all these things are subjective because they are in the subject, in me, in my mind."

"And what about objective truth? What would that be?"

"If it doesn't exist, how can it be anything?"

"I didn't ask what it *was*, only what it *would* be, if it were. What does it *mean?*"

"But can unreal things have meanings?"

"Of course. Is the term *unicorn* meaningful to you?"

"Yes."

"Do any unicorns really exist?"

"No."

"So even nonexistent things can have meaning."

"Yes."

"So what does 'objective truth' *mean*, whether it exists or not?"

"The opposite of 'subjective truth,' I suppose."

"And what would that be?"

"Something independent of me, my mind, my opinions and feelings and beliefs and desires and experiences."

"Fine. Now that we have clear and simple definitions of our terms, let us try to discover whether they exist."

"Well, subjective truth certainly exists."

"Why?"

"Because if it didn't, there wouldn't be any thoughts or opinions or feelings in my subjective consciousness at all."

"Fine. So we agree that subjective truth exists. Now what about objective truth?"

"I don't know. How can we find out whether it exists? Isn't the whole issue purely subjective? Some people believe in it and some don't. If you believe in it, it's true for you, that's all."

"Let's see whether that's all. Shall we?"

"How?"

"Let's try looking at the *consequences* of these two philosophies. If there is objective truth, then the consequence would be that our subjective truths, our opinions, could be wrong, could be out of alignment with objective truth. Isn't that so?"

"Yes. And that seems to me to be a good reason for not believing in objective truth. We could stop being judgmental and criticizing people and calling them *wrong*. They'd just be *different*."

"Yes, that would be the consequence. If there is no objective truth, then there could be no standard for judging any subjective truth as failing to conform to that standard."

"Exactly. A subjective truth—a thought—isn't *wrong*, or *false*; it just *is*."

"And therefore Protagoras's philosophy, like any other thought, just *is*. It isn't *true* or *false*."

"That necessarily follows, yes."

"And my opposite philosophy of objective truth—that too just *is*. It is not *false* any more than Protagoras's philosophy is *true*."

"Oh."

"Perhaps you would like to unpack that 'oh.' "

"It seems that subjectivism refutes itself."

"How?"

"It says that it is true that there is no truth. Or that it's objectively true that there is no objective truth."

"Wait!" interjected Protagoras.

"Good advice," replied Socrates.

"It's only subjectively true that there's no objective truth. What's wrong with that? Where's the self-contradiction in that? Nowhere!" he proclaimed triumphantly.

"But"—I struggled with the logic—"if it's only subjectively true that there's no objective truth, that only means that you have that opinion in your mind, not that you're right or that Socrates is wrong. We all agree that you have that opinion. We're not calling you a liar. Your philosophy *is* subjectively true—that is, it's yours. But I want to know whether it's objectively true. And I can't know that if there's no objective truth."

"But don't you see?" Protagoras pleaded. "That's just it. You can't know. I don't say I know it as an objective truth that there's no objective truth. I just say you can't know. See how modest I am? How nondogmatic?"

"Skepticism, then, not subjectivism," labeled Socrates.

"Yes," said Protagoras.

"But isn't that equally self-contradictory?" I put in, now getting the knack of this Socratic habit of being logical.

"How's that?" asked Protagoras.

"You now say you just don't know, right?"

"Right."

"Do you *know* that you just don't know?"

"Yes."

"Then you *do* know."

"All right then. No, I don't know."

"Then you don't claim to know that skepticism is true."

"No."

"So you're not saying that you are right and Socrates is wrong."

"No."

"Then why should I choose your path instead of his?"

Protagoras had no answer to this simple argument, and I thought that if I, a beginner, had defeated him, the most famous Sophist in Greece, that could only be either because

I was a sage or because he was a fool. And I knew I was not a sage.

I was silent for a moment, asking my mind whether it was wholly convinced. To my surprise, it was not. Then I asked why, and came up with the answer. I turned to Socrates and said, "Socrates, I am convinced that this man is a fool, but I am not yet wholly satisfied. We have shown that subjectivism is self-contradictory, but not that objective truth really exists. Our argument has been wholly negative. Is there a positive one too? What reason do we have for believing that objective truth really exists?"

"What about your own experience?"

"What do you mean?"

"Do you ever experience yourself creating subjective truths—dreams, fantasies, pictures in your mind?"

"Yes."

"And do you also experience yourself discovering objective truths that contradict the dreams and fantasies? For instance, you dream that you are in Hawaii, and then you stumble into a snowbank and you know you are in New England."

"Yes, of course."

"So you experience these two things, and the difference between them?"

"Yes."

"Would you say that is the difference between science and art?"

"I'm not sure—what do you mean by that?"

"An artist—a novelist, for instance—creates a fictional world?"

"Yes."

"And things in that world are true in that world, are they not? For instance, in *The Odyssey* there is a Cyclops, and in

The Lord of the Rings there are elves."

"Yes."

"Elves are 'true' in *The Lord of the Rings*, but not outside that fictional world."

"Yes."

"So you could call them subjective truths."

"All right."

"But objective truths are discovered, not created; by science, not art; in the real world, not in fictional worlds. Things like lobsters, and quasars, and principles like the law of gravity."

"That seems like an obvious distinction. But suppose all scientific ideas are only subjective too. Suppose science is only another form of art. Why couldn't that be so?"

"If that were so, why would we discover real dinosaur bones but never real dragon bones?"

"Ah. Yes. You can't ignore that difference."

"And it is a difference in your experience, is it not? I mean the difference between creating and discovering. The difference between making up an idea in your mind and bumping up against real things."

"Yes, but truth is not a *thing*. We want to prove objective *truth*, not just objective *things*."

"I see you are becoming more subtle and philosophical and demanding already."

"I'm sorry . . ."

"Don't be. I meant it as a compliment."

"Oh."

"So your question deserves an answer. Do you have the experience of bumping up against objective truths with your mind, as well as bumping up against objective things with your body?"

"For instance?"

"That two things plus two more always make four things. And that things fall down, not up. And that trees have leaves."

"But those are concrete *things*—trees and leaves. Truth isn't a concrete thing like a tree or a leaf."

"That is a fine distinction. Trees are material things, and leaves are material things, but the fact that trees have leaves is not a third material thing. It is a truth about those two things."

"Yes."

"And it is an objective truth. Like the truth that rocks are hard."

"Somehow I don't feel absolutely sure that such truths are objective," I admitted. I had to be totally honest with my doubts, no matter how stupid they sounded.

At this point Socrates deliberately jostled me so that my foot bumped against a large, pointed rock. "Ouch!" I cried, grabbing a bleeding toe. (We were both wearing open sandals.)

"See?" said Socrates gently. "You *do* have the experience of a world out there, a world you did not make and cannot change just by thinking about it."

I was quite convinced by now, but Protagoras, who had been biding his time, must have seen that I was about to choose to leave him forever, for he broke into the conversation with one last attempt: "How do you know you didn't do just that? How do you know you didn't change the world just by thinking about it? You can think about Socrates, can't you? Of course you can. And you can meet him, bump up against him, can't you? Of course you can. Suppose you first think about meeting him, then you meet him. Maybe the first thing *caused* the second. Maybe your thinking about him created your meeting him."

"This is getting ridiculous," I said impatiently.

But to my surprise, Socrates restrained me and said, "Patience. You must be sure. If you do not resolve all your doubts now, they will bother you later, when you are strongly tempted to *want* to believe there is no objective truth."

"What do you mean?" I asked.

"I mean when it comes to truths about good and bad, not just trees and leaves. When someone praises you for doing something good, you will want to believe it was really good, and that you really and truly deserve it, won't you?"

"Yes."

"And when someone blames you for doing something bad, you will want to believe that that truth is only subjective, only in one's mind, won't you? Isn't it at such times that you want to believe that 'there is nothing good or bad, but thinking makes it so'?"

"I suppose so."

"So we had better settle the issue for good before it comes to that, before it gets all confused with feelings and your ego and such."

"You're right. If we are honest."

"Now let us answer Protagoras. Sometimes we bump up against a thing *after* we think about it, do we not?"

"Yes."

"And sometimes we bump up against a thing *before* thinking about it, do we not? Did you want to stub your toe? Did you plan to do it? Did you worry about doing it?"

"No, I didn't. If I had thought about it first, I would have avoided it."

"So that rock, and that stub, could not have been caused by your thinking about it, because you *weren't* thinking about it."

"Oh. How simple!"

"Tell me from your own experience: what happens to your mind when you stub your toe?"

"It gets the cobwebs knocked out of it."

"You mean the dreams and fantasies and desires and false ideas, right?"

"Yes."

"Have you ever stubbed your toe on a dragon?"

"No."

"Why not? Because you never thought of dragons?"

"No. Because there are no dragons."

"I rest my case."

"Oh, you are obviously right, Socrates. As right as rain. How could anyone in his right mind choose Protagoras's way?" And with that I strode decisively away down the right fork of the road, with Socrates nodding his head in approval and Protagoras shaking his from side to side in a private prophecy of doom.

THREE

THE CYNIC

Can't We Be Cynical About Cynicism?

🔲🔲🔲🔲🔲🔲🔲🔲🔲

*A*s *we left Protagoras behind, we could see and hear him* wagging his head and tongue at us. But he did not follow us. (Apparently these philosophers that we met at each fork in our road could not leave their places and follow us.)

I cannot tell how long we walked down the rocky road toward the tiny hole in the ceiling that we had seen from afar. All I know is that it took far longer than I had expected. But eventually the road forked again, and as soon as it did, another philosopher immediately appeared in the left fork. This one, however, had no robe. He was dressed in nothing but a barrel, and he was carrying a lantern. He looked like a sad and spastic frog—rather like Jean-Paul Sartre.

"Diogenes!" called Socrates, evidently recognizing him.

"What nonsense have you come to beguile us with today? Are you still looking for an honest man with that lantern? Have you not yet noticed the holes in your barrel?"

Diogenes scowled and replied, very sternly, "I will deter your poor victim from his pointless quest."

"And how will you do that, Diogenes? You certainly do not make for a very attractive alternative."

"I will ask him how he intends to find this 'meaning of life' he is searching for. Protagoras said there is no objective truth at all, and you refuted him easily. But I am much more commonsensical. Of course there is some objective truth, and you can know it. It is self-contradictory to say otherwise. But not about the meaning of life. Physics and mathematics and such things are objective truths, but what you are looking for is objective truth in something like philosophy or religion or morality—am I right? Is that the sort of thing you are hoping to find?" He turned to me with his question.

"Yes," I said.

"Well, give it up. The meaning of life is that life has no meaning, in that sense. Or, if you prefer, the meaning is subjective. You make it up as you go along. It is whatever you please. Different strokes for different folks. For some it's philosophizing, for some it's collecting bottle caps."

I looked down at my bleeding toe as if it were some talisman against this man's spell of black magic. Noticing it, Diogenes said, "You may stub your toe against a stone, but how do you expect to stub your toe against 'the meaning of life'?"

"Not my toe," I said indignantly, "my mind."

"Ah, you think it can be found by *thinking?*"

"Yes."

"But it has not worked! Thousands have thought, and

they have come up with thousands of thoughts. Unlike stones, meanings are as manifold as we make them."

"So the meaning of life is purely subjective."

"Exactly."

"But *that* thought is also only subjective. So why should I believe it?" I thought I had learned how to refute this kind of thing.

But Diogenes had an answer: "Nearly everyone agrees about stones, do they not?"

"Yes."

"But not about the meaning of life."

"No."

"So how can you possibly say you can hope to know the objective truth about that? No matter what you believe, you will be disagreeing with the majority, and with many minds much brighter than yours."

My heart fell when I realized that Diogenes had appropriated the Socratic method and that I was on the receiving end instead of the giving end. I looked desperately to Socrates, who was standing meekly and silently beside me. He saw my look, understood, and shot back a look of his own which said both *Good for you for beginning to think and argue for yourself* and also *Too bad you have to give up so soon and ask for my help*—just like a father, easy to please and hard to satisfy. He then turned to address Diogenes.

"Let us see first whether we have understood your argument, before we decide whether to be persuaded by it. Is it fair to summarize it this way?—that whether or not there is objective truth about such things as *stones*, and whether or not we can know *that*, there is no objective truth about the meaning of life, about things we cannot touch and sense, like moral and religious and philosophical questions. Or if there *is* objective truth about the meaning of life, we cannot hope to find it and know it. This is your conclusion, is it not?"

"Yes. Things like my barrel and things like your 'meaning of life' are very, very different kinds of things."

"And how are they different?"

"Everyone can find my barrel easily, Socrates, but no one can find your so-called meaning of life."

"Is this because it is too difficult to find, since we cannot sense it with our bodies as we can sense your barrel?"

"Yes."

"Or is it because people disagree much more about the meaning of life than about your barrel?"

"That too. Both reasons. People disagree *because* it is so difficult."

At this point Socrates turned to me and put in an aside: "Note that it is always well to restate your opponent's argument in your own words to his own satisfaction, to be sure you understand it before you begin to evaluate it."

I remembered my history, and said, "Wasn't that a maxim of the medieval universities in their Scholastic Disputations?"

"It was. They really inherited that from me. It is a rule of fundamental fairness in debate. Your culture has quite forgotten it, except in the sciences. This is one reason you have so little understanding and so little agreement outside the sciences."

"It's a rule of morality, then—to be fair to your opponent?"

"Yes, but also a rule of self-interest, to be fair to yourself."

"I don't understand."

"*Why* do you debate? Is it not to find the truth? Is this not your self-interest?"

"I hope so."

"So do I. And you would not be sure what was true if the argument you refuted was not really your opponent's argument at all, but some other, some 'straw man' you had set up just to knock down. You would be like ships passing in the night rather than like crossed swords testing which blade was stronger."

"So even if I defeated the 'straw man' argument, I would not have defeated my opponent."

"I would not put it like that. I would not want to defeat my human opponent at all."

"What?"

"My real opponent is not made of flesh and blood. My opponent is ignorance, and I hope that is the opponent of my dialogue partner too. If so, we are fundamentally friends, not enemies, since we seek the same thing. This is why I seek out people who disagree with me. They are my special friends and allies. Their opposition helps me to be surer of the truth, as iron sharpens iron, or as a sparring partner strengthens your muscles, or an experiment confirms your theory."

I was grateful for this advice, and surprised that Socrates spoke directly this time like a preacher, instead of indirectly by questioning like a philosopher. Evidently this was a quasi-religious thing to him.

He then turned again to Diogenes. "Let us now examine these two reasons, the reason of Difficulty and the reason of Disagreement. Tell me, please: is it harder to discover a small stone than a large stone?"

"Of course."

"And is the small stone any less objective, or objectively true?"

"No."

"Then difficulty in discovery does not take away objective truth."

"Not a little difference like that, Socrates—between two stones. But there is a big difference between any sized stone and the meaning of life. You won't find the meaning of life no matter how good your glasses or microscopes are."

"But if difficulty of discovery made a thing more subjective, then a *little* difficulty of discovery would make the thing a *little* more subjective, and a big difficulty would make it a lot more subjective. But the little difficulty of discovering a little stone does not make the little stone even a little subjective. So the principle is not valid."

Diogenes did not answer but instead began to sulk. So Socrates tried to reason with him again. "Don't you see? How many small stones are on the surface of the moon is a very difficult thing to discover, but it is objective. Whether I feel a small stone in my shoe is a very easy thing to discover, but it is subjective. So *difficulty* and *subjectivity* are not the same."

Instead of thanking Socrates for the clarification, Diogenes sulked some more. Socrates went on (more for my sake than for Diogenes'): "And your second reason also seems to prove nothing. Disagreement is no more a criterion of subjectivity than difficulty is. May I prove that to you?"

"I can't stop you."

"No, but you can stop yourself from looking at it. Look here for a moment, please, with me. Let us look at what people do disagree about. Do people ever disagree about the size of stones?"

"Sometimes."

"About the future? For instance, when a baby will be born?"

"Yes."

"About the past? For instance, when the universe began?"

"Yes."

"And about what things are good and what things are evil?"

"Yes."

"And about the meaning of life?"

"That too."

"But are not these things objective truths? Either the universe began billions of years ago, or it didn't. Either the baby will be born tomorrow, or not. Either it is good to fight a certain war, or it is not. Either life has meaning, or it does not. Either that meaning is to find the truth, or not. Each of these things is very different from something subjective, like a feeling, that is dependent on you."

"Some of these things are feelings, Socrates. Like the meaning of life. That's why people disagree about it. It's subjective."

"We have seen, at least, that people do sometimes disagree about some objective things, have we not?"

"Yes."

"Now let us see whether they disagree about subjective things."

"All right."

"Do they disagree about whether I feel pain in my foot? Or whether you desire to drink ale?"

"No. People don't argue about those things."

"Why not?"

"They are purely subjective."

"Aha! So it is not subjective things but objective things that people argue about."

"It looks like it."

"And do people argue about things they disagree on or

things they agree on?"

"Things they disagree on."

"So disagreement is only about objective things, not subjective things."

"That seems to follow."

"So disagreement about something is a reason not for thinking that something is subjective, but rather for thinking that it is objective."

"Oh."

"Do you see? Disagreement about something does not make that something subjective."

"I guess that follows logically. But it still seems common sense to say it does."

"I think not. Does it seem common sense to say that you can turn $2 + 2 = 4$ from an objective truth into a subjective truth simply by choosing to disbelieve it? That you can change the number of years the world has existed simply by not agreeing with whatever scientists have discovered about it? That I can change the truth about your barrel just by changing my thoughts about it? That I can remove the rock in my sandal just by doubting it? Is that what you call common sense?"

"But Socrates, all these are physical things. The meaning of life is not."

"True. But your argument was that the meaning of life is subjective because people disagree about it. Was that not your argument?"

"Yes."

"And that argument needs to assume that whatever people disagree about is subjective. Is that logic correct?"

"Yes."

"And I have shown that your assumption is false. For many of the things people disagree about are objective, while people do *not* disagree about the subjective."

"All right then, it is subjective not because people disagree about it but because it is not physical."

"So whatever is not physical is not objective?"

"Yes."

"So your thoughts, which are not physical, are not objective to me, not independent of my thoughts? Your thoughts are only figments of my imagination?"

"Of course not."

"But thoughts are not physical things, are they?"

"No."

"Therefore it is not true that all nonphysical things are subjective."

"So it isn't. But the meaning of life is."

"Why? You have not yet given any good reason for your belief."

"Maybe not, Socrates, but neither have you. All you've done is refute my arguments. Give me something positive. Prove there *is* objective truth about the meaning of life."

"Suppose I could not do so. What would you conclude from that?"

"That you ought to be a cynic about it, like me, and believe that life has no meaning."

"Because I could not prove it?"

"Yes."

"So you are now assuming that we should believe only what we can prove."

"Yes. Isn't that the way *you* proceed? Isn't that *your* working assumption?"

"Certainly not!"

"But I thought you were big on this thing of reason and logic and proof."

"Oh, I am. But I don't think it's logical at all to demand

proof for everything."

"Why not?"

"Because I do not see how I can have proof of *that*."

Diogenes looked puzzled, so Socrates put it another way. "Do you say we should doubt everything we cannot prove?"

"Yes."

"Can you prove that principle?"

Diogenes looked embarrassed, as if his barrel had become transparent.

"Since you cannot prove it, we should not believe it, according to your principle. For your principle is not that 'seeing is believing' but that 'proving is believing.' All right, Diogenes, you have convinced me. You are right. Your conclusion is correct: we should not believe it if we cannot prove it. So let us abandon this unprovable principle that you must doubt whatever you can't prove. And therefore even if I can't prove that life has meaning, that will not convince me that I should doubt it. Thank you for your lesson, Diogenes."

"And thank you for yours, Socrates," I said. "I see your strategy now. Instead of trying to prove life had meaning, you disproved all the arguments that it didn't. Just like before: instead of proving objective truth, you disproved all the arguments against it. Why did you do it that way?"

"Because we all begin by believing in truth, and objective truth, and our power to know it, and even in a real meaning and purpose to life. Then along come some skeptics who give us reasons for doubting this. If I can refute all those reasons, we are back where we started, believing with no good reasons to doubt. We do not start as skeptics and then prove that there is truth. We start as believers. We assume that truth is, and is objective, and is knowable. And whenever we choose the opposite road from this assumption, we fail. On that road we embrace nonsense and contradiction: the truth that there is no truth, or the proof that there is no proof. In fact we prove only that we are fools when we try that road. But nothing proves we are fools to try the other road."

"And that is the road I will try now," I said decisively, turning my back on Diogenes.

He called out from behind me: "You will never find that wild goose that you chase!"

"Perhaps not," I called back to him. "But even if not, the chase is worth the effort. Common sense itself tells me so. 'Better to have loved and lost than never to have loved at all.' 'Nothing ventured, nothing gained.' The mere search for this truth is worth more than all that you offer me."

"What makes you think you are so different from me that you will find it? What do you think you've got that I haven't got?"

The direct question demanded a direct answer. "Courage to venture," I said. "And curiosity. How will I ever know if I do not try?"

"You'll be back!" he predicted glumly.

But by now I realized that it was time to stop arguing with him. "Goodby," I said—more with my feet than my mouth.

As we walked down the right road, Socrates asked me, "Do you really think you have shown great courage?"

"Why not?" I asked.

"Courage comes only in the face of risk, does it not?"

"Yes."

"What have you risked? You yourself said it is better to travel down this road, even if you never arrive at your goal, than to arrive at the goal of his road. You have risked nothing. You have dared nothing, except to have made the daring step of believing that one philosophy of life is really truer than another—that seeking truth, for instance, is really more meaningful than collecting bottle caps. Now do you think that is a great thing for which to be praised?"

"No, it is mere sanity," I said.

"Nevertheless I praise you for it," he said. "In an insane asylum like your world, simple sanity can be a heroic achievement."

FOUR

THE NIHILIST

Is the Meaning of Life That Life Is Meaningless?

𒐫𒐫𒐫𒐫𒐫𒐫𒐫𒐫𒐫

The tiny glimmer of sunlight to which we now directed our travels looked deceptively close, and the road was straight, yet it was so far away that many hours passed before we reached our goal. But finally there it was: a hole in the rocky ceiling, easily wide enough for one to squeeze through. There was no slant; we would need to make a direct vertical ascent. Then I noticed a second hole on the floor directly under the hole in the ceiling, a mirror image of the other hole.

As Socrates and I contemplated the problem of where to stand for leverage to lift ourselves up into the ceiling hole, a man's head suddenly popped out of the floor hole, surrounded by a pair of shoulders encased in a Greek robe like those worn by Epicurus and Protagoras. "Gorgias!" called Socrates. "What are you doing here?"

"This is my home, Socrates."

"What is this place?" I asked.

"It's called Nihil House," Gorgias answered. "It is the home of all true seekers."

"It looks awfully cramped," I noted suspiciously, looking down the hole.

"Not at all," retorted Gorgias cheerfully. "Down there it opens up into vast vistas."

"It also looks dry," I said, suddenly feeling thirsty.

"Oh no," said Gorgias. "It's fed by the greatest of rivers."

"The Nihil River, no doubt?" Socrates commented dryly.

"Of course," said Gorgias. "The water of wisdom. Come down and see it. Drink from it. This is the real truth about the meaning of life. You were right to seek one step further than Diogenes' place. You can indeed find the objective truth about the meaning of life. It is here. Wisdom is here."

"What wisdom?" I asked.

"The wisdom of unwisdom," he answered. "The meaning of unmeaning. The true meaning of life. It is that life is meaningless. Back in Greece I summarized my wisdom in three maxims. First, nothing is really real. Second, if it were, we could not know it. Third, if we could, we could not communicate it. In other words, deep down everything is shallow—empty, like an inflated balloon, once you get beneath the surface scrim. There's your true metaphysics, your worldview. And even if there *were* anything solid and substantial, our minds are too weak and uncertain to be able to know it. There's your true epistemology, your theory of knowledge. And even if someone could know it, it would be a purely private experience, and no one, not even Socrates, could lead anyone else there. There's your true linguistics and methodology. These three truths together are your true enlightenment. True enlightenment consists in not expecting any light from life."

"You mean that light up there"—I pointed to the hole in the ceiling—"that world up there—it's all a fake?"

"Exactly."

"Who else lives down there with you?" I asked.

"The greatest of sages," Gorgias replied. "Solomon and Sartre and Nietzsche and Beckett, for instance. Even Buddha drops by on Sundays. Tolstoy was here for a while, but left."

"I read about that in his *Confessions*," I said. "Well, you certainly do have an impressive crowd down there."

"In quality, yes. Not, of course, in quantity. Many sages but few peasants. And that's another selling point. It's not overcrowded, and your neighbors would be the intellectual elite."

"But why would so many sages choose a hole in the ground to settle in? Why did they all conclude that life is really meaningless?"

"From experience," replied Gorgias confidently. "Old Solomon, for instance. Have you read Ecclesiastes? He tried everything—and I do mean everything—and found it all 'vanity of vanities'—wine, women and song; money, sex and power; honor, fame and glory; even duty and altruism and social service. Even obeying the law and going to church."

"But did he really try everything?" I asked.

"Oh yes," Gorgias assured me, then turned to Socrates. "Even your path, Socrates—I mean philosophy, the search for wisdom. And he found only that 'in much wisdom is much sorrow,' and that 'of the making of many books there is no end, and much study is a weariness.' "

"It seems more like a mood than a philosophy," I observed. "I'm sorry, Gorgias, but I'm just not as hopeless as that. Not yet, anyway. Not till I've tested and retested whether old Solomon was right in thinking he had tried everything. Maybe he missed the real meaning of life. Did he try love, for instance?"

"I'll say he did!" answered Gorgias. "He had seven hundred wives."

Socrates put in a word at this point. "He didn't ask you about sex, Gorgias; he asked you about love."

Gorgias's face took on a look of blank perplexity.

"Look here," I put in impatiently, feeling the need for decision rather than argument. "I have no reason to linger here. I intend to try to find a way up out of this miserable rabbit hole into the sun outside. So please stand aside—unless you have something to say to me that has the authority of reason behind it instead of the authority of yourself and your elitist pessimist friends."

Socrates gave me a quick proud father's look, for I was not only standing up for myself and talking back but also appealing to the authority of reason—the only authority that he knew never enslaved but always liberated.

Gorgias must have realized I was beyond any appeal but that. For he said to me sweetly, "Come now, let us reason together. How do you expect to recognize the meaning of life if you ever do find it? What method will you use? What standard will you measure it by? Not logic, not mathematics, not physics—what? And how do you know your method and your standard are valid?"

But I did not allow myself to be sucked into his gambit. "I do not need to answer those questions in order to search for the meaning of life," I replied. "I do not need to justify human reason before using it to find the truth about life. You are distracting me from my question and from my quest."

"But how do you expect to do it?"

"Even if I don't know *how* I do it, I may still do it. We often figure out how we did a thing only after we do it rather than before."

"But you are being uncritical. You are not critically evaluating your tool, reason, before using it. How untrue to the spirit of Socrates, your guide!"

At this point Socrates interjected some help. "It is you, Gorgias, who are uncritical. You uncritically assume that we must always be critical, without criticizing *that* assumption."

"But you are like a carpenter who builds a house without being sure his tools are sharp enough to cut wood," protested Gorgias. "That is not reasonable."

Socrates replied, "But if examining the tools is a substitute for building the house, then that examination is not reasonable."

"Right, Socrates," I said. "At least I'm making some progress toward my goal. Gorgias isn't. I don't know *how* I'm doing it, but I'm doing it. So I'm better off than he is."

"But you're *naive!*" Gorgias spat out the word as a devout Muslim would spit out the word *alcohol!*

"If being naive is the price of going somewhere, I'll pay it," I said, and turned decisively away. As soon as I did, Gorgias disappeared down into his hole.

Socrates grinned.

"What are you grinning about?" I asked.

"I've just witnessed the history of modern philosophy," he said. "And your escape from its stranglehold."

FIVE

THE MATERIALIST

What's the Matter with "Nothing But Matter"?

⛩⛩⛩⛩⛩⛩⛩⛩⛩

*N*ow *how shall we get up this hole?" I asked. The shaft in*
the rock was wide enough to climb through and narrow
enough to wedge oneself in to prevent falling, but neither
of us could reach its opening without standing on something. One of us would have to squat over Gorgias's hole,
as over a toilet bowl, so that the other could stand on him.

Socrates observed, "If I stand on you, you will be left
behind, and if you stand on me, I will be left behind.
Therefore it seems that this is where I must leave you.
You've been doing quite well by yourself lately anyway,
and it is your journey, after all; I am only your temporary
guide."

As I prepared sadly to thank Socrates and leave him by

climbing up on his shoulders into the shaft of light, some-thing suddenly slid down the shaft and filled it, blocking my exit. It was another man wearing a Greek robe. He was hairy, dark, large and very fat, and he hung upside down in the shaft, nose toward the dusty floor and feet kicking at the sky. He blocked the shaft completely, so that not a glimmer of daylight shone through.

"Democritus!" called Socrates in recognition. "Up to your old tricks again, I see."

Democritus ignored him and called down to me, "You may as well turn back. There is no other world up there. There is only more of the same—rocks and caves, just like down here."

"But what about the light, and the sun, and the air?"

"Superstition!" said Democritus. "I can explain it all. Forms of rock and dirt, that's all. Forms of matter. Matter is all that is, all that matters. Never mind mind. Only matter matters."

"No mind? No spirit? No self? No soul? Nobody home here?" I asked, pointing to my head.

"Nothing but gray matter," he said. "Your 'mind' is nothing but your brain. No spooks, no spirits—not in your head, and not in your world, and not beyond it. Not in your head, because what's there is blood and bones and tissue. Not in your world, because what's there is rocks and dirt. Not beyond it, because there *is* no 'beyond,' no space beyond space and no time beyond time. There's no place for gods to be. This is all there is, there ain't no more. What you see is what you get . . ."

As much to stop his torrent of slogans as to argue with his philosophy, I objected, "But what about thinking?"

"Brain activity," he answered breezily. "Nothing more. The working of your built-in computer."

"But who programmed it?"

"Wind, weather, digestion, natural selection, chance—take your pick. But matter, it has to be matter. That's all there is."

Disconcerted, I was unsure how to attack this claim. So Socrates came to my aid again. "Tell me, Democritus, do you really mean that my mind is nothing else at all than my brain? Not one wee little thing more?"

"Not one thing, Socrates."

"And it is like a computer?"

"Yes."

"And it is programmed only by matter, since that is all there is?"

"Yes."

"Then tell me why I should trust it, even now. Who would trust a computer programmed by chance instead of intelligence? By matter instead of mind? By a hailstorm instead of a human? Why should I trust it even if it tells me that Democritus's philosophy is true?"

"You have no choice, Socrates. Matter has caused us to think whatever we think, and to happen whatever happens."

"In your brain as well as mine, Democritus?"

"Certainly."

"And you are trying to convince me that this philosophy of yours is true?"

"Yes."

"What do you mean by 'true'?"

"It corresponds to the facts."

"And the facts are all the states and events of matter? That's all there is?"

"Exactly."

"Then what is it that corresponds to these facts, if the

facts are all there is? I thought you said there *was* nothing else."

"My thoughts are simply some more facts. Brain chemistry."

"Like one of many leaves on a tree."

"Exactly."

"So if the universe were a tree, and if there were a thousand leaves on the tree, my thought would be one of those leaves."

"Yes."

"And a philosophy is a thought, or a series of thoughts?"

"Yes."

"And you say your philosophy is true and mine is false?"

"Yes."

"So you say your thought is true and mine is false."

"That's what I say."

"And you say a thought is true if it corresponds to the facts, and false if it does not?"

"Yes."

"Now suppose there are two trees in my yard. Let's say one has small leaves and the other has large leaves. Would you say that one tree is 'true' and the other tree is 'false'? Or would you rather say that the *idea* that the tree with large leaves has large leaves is true, and the opposite idea is false?"

"Ideas about leaves are true or false, but not leaves themselves."

"Well, then, don't you see what follows? If material things are like leaves and are neither true nor false, and if ideas *are* either true or false, then ideas are not just material things."

"But that would mean there are things that are not material!"

"Exactly."

"That cannot be."

"That seems to be your unquestioned faith. But it is not rational. It is faith rather than reason. It may be a religion, but it is not philosophy."

"Religion? I despise religion! That's all silly superstition."

"Hmmm . . . say, have you ever looked in a mirror?"

As Democritus hung from the ceiling stewing, I decided that I was quite convinced by Socrates' simple and obvious argument. "Move out of our way, Democritus. We will not be blocked by your silly superstition."

As soon as I said this, to my surprise Democritus plopped down out of the shaft, allowing light once more to enter, and lay in a large lump on the ground next to Gorgias's hole, thereby solving our problem of leverage for our climb. We simply climbed atop his now-unmoving body and lifted ourselves into the exit shaft. Apparently the guardians of the gates, or forks in the road, were surprisingly subject to my will.

As I followed Socrates up the shaft, I turned to look at Democritus. As he lay there, he took on different forms, some of which I recognized as Darwin, Marx and Freud. "What a large family he has!" I exclaimed to Socrates. "Why has his materialistic idea had such popular progeny, I wonder? It's such a low, depressing and insulting idea that there is no spirit, no soul, no self, except matter. Why are so many intellectuals in my culture attracted to it?"

"Why do *you* think?" asked Socrates.

Taking up his challenge, I thought for a moment, then said: "I think it is because it offers exculpation from guilt."

"What do you mean?"

"Only a self can be guilty, because only a self can be morally responsible. If we are nothing but clever apes, as Darwin says, or pawns of our economic system, as Marx says, or bundles of sex urges, as Freud says, then there is no free moral agent to blame, and no one to feel guilty. Morality becomes a myth." The more I thought about the connection, the more sense it made. "And that is why Marxists are always justifying things like propaganda and purges of politically incorrect dissidents, in the state or the university. And why Freudians will never condemn any misbehavior, only try to understand its necessary causes. And why Darwinians explain aggression and ruthless competition and selfishness as the territorial imperatives of animals. All three are materialisms, and materialism removes the soul, and therefore free will, and therefore moral responsibility, and therefore guilt. That's why people are attracted to these philosophies."

"And what about you?" continued Socrates. "Are you attracted to them too?"

"No," I said.

"Why not?"

"Because that seems too high a price to pay just to get even with guilt. 'What does it profit a man to gain the whole world but lose his own soul?' It's a kind of spiritual euthanasia: killing the patient to cure the disease, losing the soul to lose the guilt."

But my philosophical musings were cut short by reality, as we suddenly found ourselves no longer underground but standing in the outside world, blinking in strong sunlight.

SIX

THE RELATIVIST

Is It Really Wrong to Think There's a Real Right & Wrong?

丗丗丗丗丗丗丗丗丗

*N*ow *that's more like it!" I exclaimed, and started off at once*
down the road in the bright sunlight and fresh air. Socrates,
however, held back, and after a few steps I turned to find
him sitting down beside the hole we had climbed up.

I returned to him, puzzled, and asked, "Why the hesi-
tation, Socrates? There is no fork in the road here."

"But there is a choice to be made," he said.

"You mean the choice to travel or not to? I have already
made that, long ago. Why won't you come along? What
other choice is there here?"

"Have you forgotten what a road is?" he asked. "A road
always has two directions, not one."

To my embarrassment, I saw that I had indeed forgotten
this. The hole from which we had emerged was at the side of
a road that led in two directions. I had unthinkingly followed

it to the left, since it sloped gradually *down* in that direction and *up* in the other. I also saw that the downward road was much broader and easier, whereas it seemed to get increasingly narrow to the right, where it wound up a small mountain.

Embarrassment at my past thoughtlessness and my present uncertainty paralyzed my feet and my future. I wondered what this new choice signified and how I was to discern it. As soon as my mind formulated this question, my world provided the answer. A man who looked very much like Democritus, only smaller and younger, climbed out of our hole and wildly gestured to us to take the left road. "That way! That way!" he shouted.

"Thrasymachus!" called Socrates. "I haven't seen you since that day in Ariston's house when we had that long conversation about justice."

"Whatever came of that conversation, Socrates?" asked Thrasymachus.

"Why, that young upstart Plato added to it all sorts of political nonsense of his own and then peddled it as *my* ideas, and it seems to have become quite famous."

"I suppose he made you out to be right all the time, as usual?"

"I'm afraid so."

"And me to be wrong?"

"Yes."

"Well, I've failed twice to sell my philosophy: to you, and to Plato. May I try a third time, to your friend here?"

As I nodded my permission, Socrates replied, "That is your function, Thrasymachus. Tell us, where do you say this road leads, and how should we follow it?"

"To the right it leads to the land of law; to the left it leads to the land of liberty."

"Strange," said Socrates. "The only way *I* know to reach the land of liberty is to take the road of law."

"That's your mistake, Socrates. You think the laws that label some deeds good and others evil are 'out there' somewhere, like the stars. But they are *our* laws, Socrates. They are not the laws of nature, like gravity or the seasons. There is no natural law of good and evil, as you thought. There may be objective *truth,* but there is no objective *goodness.*"

"No real right and wrong, then?"

"No."

"Only our will, our desires?"

"Yes."

"Then we cannot be wrong about right and wrong."

"No, Socrates, not really. The one who *makes* the law is not *under* it, but over it."

"And that one is the individual person?"

"Or the collective person, the State. Insofar as individuals make a state, they are above the State and can change it—and often do. Insofar as the State makes individuals what they are, teaching them its laws, it is above them. It has the power to make us believe as it wishes us to believe about good and evil. Democratic states make us believe that democracy is good. Monarchical states make us believe that monarchy is good. That's the way it is. Whoever has the power makes the laws and defines justice and good and evil."

"In other words, might makes right."

"It sounds shocking, but it is true."

"And this philosophy of yours, Thrasymachus—that there is no natural law of good and evil—this is the philosophy that you say leads to the land of liberty?"

"Yes indeed. It is the bold, progressive way, the way of

the enlightened rebel like myself. The other way is the way of the unthinking majority, the stodgy traditionalists, the stuck-in-the-mud conservatives like yourself."

"I am aware that most people think in these categories," said Socrates, "since they are universally taught this way by universities and journalists and entertainment—the three main mind-molding establishments in today's society. But in fact it must be just the opposite, if you only take a moment to think about it. It is *your* road that leads to the status quo, and it is the other road, and only that one, that can justify the progressive and the rebel."

"What nonsense is this, Socrates?"

"I believe it is called logic. Would you like a free lesson?"

"All right, what clever sophism do you have up your sleeve now?"

"Only the simplest and most obvious truism. If, as you say, there is no higher law of good and evil than the law of the State, then the individual or group is never right in rebelling or changing it. If the State creates the right, it can never be right to oppose the State. How can it be right to oppose God? If the State is God, if there is nothing higher, how can it ever be right to oppose the State?"

"So you are saying I am really a status quo conservative instead of a rebel?"

"Precisely. But if you only admitted to a Higher Law, you could stand on it and criticize your society—you could be a good rebel. As it is, you can only be a bad rebel or a good conformist."

"I see it now!" I exclaimed. "That's what got Senators Kennedy and Metzenbaum and Biden so terrified at the Clarence Thomas hearings: his belief in the Natural Law. That was the real issue; Anita Hill was just a soap-opera diversion."

The two philosophers ignored me and went on. "But suppose the State is the people instead of the king," objected Thrasymachus. "Suppose it's a democracy."

"Then the majority create the right, instead of the king, and it can never be right to oppose the majority. Minorities are always in the wrong. So what becomes of your noble, bold rebel now, O Thrasymachus? You have just proved that the rebel is never noble."

Thrasymachus seemed to choke for a second, whether with rage or embarrassment or both. Then he blushed— just as Socrates had made him blush that day in Athens— and I knew the battle was over, for Socrates had already defeated his weakest part, his mind, and now he had also defeated his strongest part, his pride.

But Socrates was not yet satisfied. He went on: "Thrasymachus, you believe that the moral law is created rather than discovered, is that right? That it is man-made?"

"Yes. That is what I contend. We don't discover it as we would that mountain over there. Do you say we do?"

"That is exactly what I say. In fact, do you know the name of that mountain?"

"No. What difference does it make?"

"That is Mount Sinai."

"Oh." I thought Thrasymachus would blush again. But he did not. Instead he continued his argument. "But morality is not made of rocks, Socrates. It is made of laws. And we do not discover it with our eyes or our feet."

"True," said Socrates, "We discover it with our mind . . ."

"Socrates, I will prove that we do not. I will defeat you at your own game of proof."

"It is no game, but go ahead."

"If morality were simply 'there,' we would not create it.

But we do create it. Therefore it is not simply 'there.' Further, if morality were simply 'there,' we could not change it. But we can change it. Therefore it is not simply 'there.' Now how's that for logic?"

"Congratulations, Thrasymachus. I see you have at least learned to embrace the logical form of my philosophy, if not the content, since I saw you last. This makes it an easier and clearer and shorter task to examine whether you are right."

"I certainly hope so," I interjected. "Frankly, I'm getting a little tired of all these abstract logical arguments."

Socrates lifted an eyebrow in surprise at my words, like Mr. Spock. Then he said, gently but firmly, "Do you realize what is at stake here?"

"I guess not," I admitted.

"If there is any fork in our road that is crucial for you and your world, it is this one."

"Why is that? And how do you know so much about my world, by the way?"

"I will not answer your second question now, for that is only a matter of curiosity. But I will answer the first. For one thing, it is about nothing less than how we should live. For another thing, it most sharply distinguishes your two cities, the two societies you live in."

"Two? I thought we lived in one."

"What makes a city—a society or a community—*one?*"

"Agreement, I think. Agreement about the goals we all agree to strive for together, and about the rules that regulate the striving."

"Excellent answer. Then how could there be a single city if the masters disbelieve in the goal that the citizens believe in, and if they do not even believe the rules are permanent but can be changed at will?"

"Is that how you would describe my society?"

"It matters little what *I* say. But this is how your own world describes itself. The polls reveal it. The masters and the masses have philosophies as radically different as those of cattle ranchers and cows. For the masses still believe in the natural moral law, in an objective and unchangeable truth about good and evil. The masters do not. So it is a nation of believers taught by a faculty of unbelievers. As one of your sociologists has put it, you are a nation of Indians ruled by an elite of Swedes."

"Oh come now. Surely you are exaggerating."

"Let us see. How many people in your society think religion is important enough to practice somewhat regularly? How many attend religious services?"

"The majority. More than half, I think."

"Correct. And now let us look at your masters and teachers. I mean those in the upper echelons of your three most influential establishments: higher education, entertainment and journalism. How often do they . . ."

"Wait—these are not the most influential institutions. State and Church are."

"I think not. For those two are not entrenched in power, as the three mind-molders are. For you can vote State leaders out of office, and no church is required of you. But you cannot choose your school, unless you are rich. And you do not elect your TV producers or moviemakers or journalists."

"I see. All right, let's look at these mind-molders."

"Now among these, how many are religious?"

"I don't know."

"Well, I do. Nine percent."

"Only nine? How do you know?"

"I read polls. Don't you?"

I said nothing. He went on, "Perhaps your teachers have not wanted to make such statistics about themselves known to their students."

"That's only religion. What about morality? Surely we have a common morality, even though we have no common religion."

"Let's see," said Socrates again. "Let's look at the most passionately controversial moral issue in your society. How many people in your society think that abortion is somehow wrong and should be regulated or discouraged or even forbidden by law in some cases?"

"More than half, I think."

"Between seventy and eighty percent, according to the polls. And now, how many people in your mass media hold that opinion?"

"I don't know. What do the polls say?"

"Three percent."

"Three?"

"Three."

"That can't be right."

"Really? Tell me, when was the last time you saw a motion picture that was 'prolife' instead of 'prochoice'?"

"Mmmmm . . . maybe you're right. Wait, what about *Alfie?*"

"Which TV networks dare to show that any more?"

"I see your point. Say, how do you know so much about our society twenty-four centuries after your death?"

"I will not let you be distracted by answering that now. But do you see the point? Your teachers are moral subjectivists, their students are not—not yet anyway. The masses keep resisting the missionary efforts of their teachers to convert them to the new religion of moral relativism."

"I see. The teachers are advanced far ahead of the

students."

" 'Advanced' indeed. But is it advanced enlightenment, like a sage, or advanced decay, like a rotten tooth? You see, this question of who is more 'advanced' or 'progressive' is the way your media dodges the substantive issue. You try to tell the truth with a clock instead of an argument. That's as silly as trying to tell time with a syllogism."

"We assume that we progress more and more toward truth."

"An assumption you yourself do not believe."

"Why do you say that?"

"Would you not all admit that some old ideas are right and some are wrong?"

"Yes."

"And that some new ideas are right and some are wrong?"

"Yes."

"Then there is no necessary connection between being right and being new."

"I see."

"Now that that red herring is disposed of, let us answer Thrasymachus's two arguments. He has learned patience since I last saw him, and is waiting silently for our answer. Thrasymachus, you say that we create moral laws?"

"Yes."

"And so morality is like art rather than science, since art creates and science discovers?"

"Yes."

"Now let us see whether this is so. When you rescue a woman from a rapist, are you writing the rules or are you obeying them?"

"What do you mean?"

"Do you *make* rape wrong by hating and opposing it?"

"Why not? Perhaps I do."

"Then you would make it right by loving and desiring it."

"No, that can't be right."

"So we *do* discover some moral laws."

Thrasymachus did not know what to say to this. Socrates went on: "And your second argument was that we can change moral rules, was it not?"

"Yes. For instance, a political revolution does that."

"But those are political rules. We are now speaking of moral rules."

"Maybe that's all morality is: politics."

"Then we are back in our old problem about the rebel never being justified."

"Oh. But are you saying we can't change moral rules at all then?"

"That's exactly what I am saying."

"That's ridiculous."

"Let's see. Suppose we try. Suppose we decree that murder, theft, perjury, treason, rape, torture and adultery become good, and charity, justice, honesty and fidelity become evil. Can we do that? Can we create a new morality?"

"Some tyrants have done just that."

"No. They have created a hell on earth, but they have not created a new morality. Do we turn hell into heaven just by approving it?"

"Socrates, you sound like a preacher. You're trying to make me feel guilty and blush again. But I won't. I won't accept your oppressive moral law. I have liberated myself from guilt. There's my final argument, if argument it must be. Your objective morality still believes in guilt."

"So if there is no guilt, you are right, and if there is guilt, I am right."

"Yes."

"But there *is* guilt!"

"Not for me."

"Yes, for you too, Thrasymachus. For if guilt did not bother you, you would not want to end it, by ending the morality that causes it."

"But it is only a myth, a fiction, a fear. *That* is what I want to end: a bad dream. And when it is ended, people will no longer be judgmental, like you."

"Because then no one will be morally wrong about anything?"

"Yes."

"But sometimes people *are* wrong."

"Says you, you judgmental old moralist!"

"No; says *you,* I think. Thrasymachus, suppose I say that you have proved that you are right, that you have convinced me that morality is only a man-made thing, but I am going to bow down to it anyway and worship it as if it were the voice of God, and I will feel guilty whenever I transgress it, and I shall teach others to do the same. What would you say about me then?"

"That you are a fool, Socrates. And a lying fool at that."

"So I would then be *wrong?* Really wrong?"

"Uh-oh. There's that word again."

"See? If, as you hold, 'there is nothing right or wrong but thinking makes it so,' then if I *think* it's not really wrong to be dishonest and to lie and to teach that to others, then it's *not* really wrong. So why are you so 'judgmental' against me then? In fact, why are you 'judgmental' against me now for my being 'judgmental'? Why are you preaching if you have no faith?"

"You tie me up in knots, Socrates!"

"No, you tie yourself, Thrasymachus. I only try to untie

you. Here, let me try one more time. Do you say it is really right to seek and teach the truth, or not?"

"Nothing is really right or wrong."

"Then why do you bow so meekly to the moral law in preaching what you think is the truth of moral subjectivism?"

"All right then, it *is* right to tell the truth, as I am doing."

"Then there is something really right: what you are doing."

"Let it be so."

"But what you are doing is teaching that there is nothing really right or wrong!"

"Socrates, you are a great sophist."

"I would much rather be a poor philosopher than a great sophist, Thrasymachus. But can't you see the point? It's really very simple. Do you think it is *good* for you to liberate naive traditionalists from their supine superstition of dogmatic moral absolutism, or not?"

"Yes!"

"Then there is something really good: that."

"No, then."

"Then why do it? For power, or self-gratification?"

"Yes, that's all."

"Then why not be honest and tell us that, so we can ignore you and save our own minds and souls and integrity? Why lie to us and pretend you are doing something good, or true, or right?"

"Socrates, you are a regular garbageman of guilt. You make me feel like some low and dirty thing, like a rag."

"My services to humanity are many."

"Very funny."

"I was not joking."

"What service do you render by defending guilt?"

"The service of enlightenment."

"How do you figure *that?*"

"Is it not the function of guilt to enlighten us that we are in the wrong?"

"No. It makes us feel bad, like a toothache."

"But even a toothache enlightens us. It points to a truth: that there is something wrong with that tooth. It is tooth truth."

"So pain is good? Is this what you think?"

"Of course! If we dulled all our pain nerves, we would soon die. We would not pull our bodies out of fires. And if we dull our consciences, as you do with your philosophy of moral subjectivism, then our souls will soon die."

"I thought you taught that souls were immortal and could never die."

"That's even worse, then! They would get more and more diseased forever!"

"You know what I need after talking to you, Socrates? A bath, a shower. A shrink, I think."

"A shrink may indeed shrink your conscience, as a drug may shrink your pain nerves. A shrink may take away your guilt *feelings*, but he cannot take away your guilt, any more than a drug can take away the disease that causes the pain."

At this point Thrasymachus seemed to be getting ready to fight Socrates with his fists instead of words. I interrupted, out of pity for Thrasymachus's recent defeat at the hands of Socrates' argument, and out of pity for Socrates' impending defeat at the argument of Thrasymachus's hands, which he now held like a boxer's. "Socrates, I have chosen. I will follow you, not him. I choose the high road. Let's go."

To my surprise, Socrates hesitated. "Good," he said. "But we should be sure it is for the right reason. Remember,

'The last temptation is the greatest treason: To do the right thing for the wrong reason.' "

"And what might be the wrong reason?"

"A reason of personal association. To choose your road only to associate with familiar friends, to let them make your choices for you. I will not be that to you. Have you decided to follow truth, or Socrates? To reject error, or this miserable cur Thrasymachus?"

As I looked at Thrasymachus, he seemed to turn into a hundred academics, psychologists and writers that I recognized as my world's intellectual establishment, now revealed as a mangy little dog.

I said, "I will be a moralist like you, Socrates—not because of you but because of truth. Even my family's old-fashioned philosophy—I will follow it not because it is theirs but because it is true. But I think your way to truth is only one among many ways, Socrates. Your way is the way of impersonal reason. I think the way of personal example is at least as valid, and much more effective than all your clear, bright arguments. Do you disagree?"

"No," he said. "I do not quarrel with other roads to truth. I only offer my own."

I went on, "And even the road of fear—the fear of evil—is not that a valid road to truth? If Thrasymachus's philosophy of moral relativism is taught, it will be learned, and believed, and lived, and if it is lived it will destroy society—exactly as it is doing among us. Surely no one but a professor could be as blind as to fail to see the connection between the philosophy of doing your own thing and the social facts of doing things like drugs and rapes and murders and broken promises and broken families."

Socrates said nothing to contradict this. Indeed, he looked rather proudly at me, for choosing the right, and for doing it myself. And as I walked up the right path with Socrates, I was happy in both mind and heart, though our path was not the easy one.

As we wound our way up the increasingly narrow mountain road, I asked Socrates, "Why didn't you get into the usual arguments about moral subjectivism—for instance, that different cultures have different moral values?"

"Because although these arguments are very common, they are very shallow and easy to answer, and I thought you too wise to be disturbed by them."

"Perhaps you were wrong there. For instance, how do you refute cultural relativism?"

"By pointing out that it is a simple factual lie. If you take the time to honestly examine different cultures, you will find a nearly universal consensus on the most important moral principles, a sort of universal ten commandments. What culture values lying and adultery and murder and theft? Which one rewards traitors and punishes philanthropists?"

"None that I know of."

"And even if there were one, that would not mean it was as right as all others. Does anyone seriously believe Hitler's society was as right as Churchill's?"

"Do you really think all the standard arguments for subjectivism are answered as simply as that?"

"Yes."

"Perhaps you should take the time to show me."

"Perhaps *you* should take the time some day to read a little book I inspired called *The Best Things in Life,* by the same author I am now inspiring to write the account of this journey."

I resolved to do just that if the road ever led to a bookstore.

SEVEN

THE ATHEIST

Can There Be a Moral Law Without a Moral Lawgiver?

The road then became increasingly mountainous. *Precipitous* cliffs rose before us at every turn. The Alpine heights made me tremble with fear and awe, the cold made me shiver, and the thinness of the air made me breathe in gasps, as if I were having a fit.

As we approached the summit, I exclaimed, more to myself than to Socrates, "What a lonely place this is!" Never had I uttered a word that seemed more obviously true, yet never had I uttered a word that proved more profoundly false. As soon as I spoke, as if in answer, there came the most terrifying thing my eyes had ever seen.

It was as if the entire sky turned into a single immense lightning bolt that was frozen in time. I felt an electricity in depths of my body that I had never suspected even existed.

The lightning was far brighter than any light I had ever seen, yet it did not hurt my eyes.

Then came the thunder. As the booming of gigantic waves and the screaming of hurricane winds are to the plink of a pebble in a puddle, so was this thunder to a hurricane. The whole earth became a giant drum. All of China became a gong. The sound seemed bigger than the universe, yet it did not burst my eardrums.

Then came the fire. It was as if the whole world had fallen into the heart of the sun. And yet my flesh was not seared. But when the foolish thought entered my heart that I must have become superhumanly strong to endure such things, there came immediately the thing that sent me whimpering in terror like a dog or a tiny baby.

It was a still, small voice, clear as the air on the day of creation, infinitely far away yet at the same time infinitely close. Like me, Socrates fell flat on his face as one dead. I saw his body glow with a terrible light, like St. Elmo's fire. Then I saw that mine was glowing too.

No words came from either of us. Nor did words come *to* us. For a single Word had overtaken all words and eaten them as a whale eats microscopic plankton. Even the word *God,* when it bubbled to my lips, burst and died there.

I had anticipated from the beginning of my journey that we would at some time reach the fork in the road where I would have to choose between theism and atheism. And I had thought that choice would be like the others: safe, detached and intellectual. I had thought I would see all the great old arguments trotted out—the First Cause Argument on the one side versus the Problem of Evil on the other, for instance. But I was not to walk down those well-trodden and comfortable roads, not even with Socrates.

It was not *argument* I was confronted with, but Reality. And the choice was elementally simple: I could go back, in fear—the most natural thing in the world—or I could go forward, in hope—the craziest, most radical thing in the world. If I went forward, over the summit of this mountain, I could be in for *anything*. The Thing I confronted was not even a verbal Voice; but whatever It was, It clearly demanded: "All!"

The choice was excruciating. It was more like subtracting than adding, more like a snake shedding its whole skin than like a coward becoming a hero. No courage helped me to endure it. The only thing in me that could endure this total Power was total weakness.

I found out in that moment that all my life, with incredible folly, I had thought the essential religious choice—to believe in, to hope in and to love this transcendent Mystery—would be like a multiple-choice test in school, or like buying food in a supermarket or ordering it in a restaurant. Instead it was like going back to a pink, shivering, quivering little thing that has just emerged from its mother's womb, naked and defenseless.

The only positive thing in me that enabled me to choose to go on at that point was certainly not my courage, or even my curiosity, but my fanatical and irrational demand for Truth No Matter What. "Though Truth slay me, yet will I trust him," I said, and stepped forward. To be slain by truth was better than to be given life by Falsehood.

In light of this Light I was a mass of maggots; the Light would kill them inexorably and instantly, and I had no idea what would then remain in me. Quite possibly nothing at all. As I stepped forward, I felt nothing at all like a lover going to his bride, more like a martyr going to his stake, but most like a criminal going to his electric chair.

Socrates walked along with me, but he seemed no longer the teacher—more like a swimmer out far beyond his depth, like me. I had chosen to surf a giant wave with no assurance against total wipeout or even of survival. I walked toward the Light for the same reason Hilary had climbed Everest: because it was There, because it was True.

As we walked over the summit and prepared to go down the other side of the mountain, the lightning, the thunder, the fire and the still, small voice all withdrew. I dared to turn around for a last look at the road we had taken up to this summit. There, a little way down, I noticed a wild-eyed man dancing along the path. We must have passed him without seeing him. It was Xenophanes (Socrates identified him to me). The man gestured gently with his finger, pointing to the sky, then to his head, sadly shaking "no"—but he soon turned into Nietzsche, who was thrusting his fist against the air and screaming: "No! No! No!" in endless and eternal trinitarian parody.

How could I have failed to notice this madman? I wondered. Then I remembered the Light and the Voice, and that question was answered.

It seemed superfluous to try to answer Nietzsche. He was not arguing, so it was impossible to argue with him. Instead he was repeating his mantra: "I will now disprove the existence of all gods. If there were gods, how could I bear not to be a god? *Consequently*, there are no gods."

I heard the sarcasm in the word *consequently* and was wise enough not to play his hellish game. It reminded me of Satan's famous line from *Paradise Lost:* "Better to reign in Hell than serve in Heaven." As we left him, his voice turned into Sinatra's, crooning "I Did It My Way."

Once we were down the awful mountain and on level ground, I was able to speak to Socrates again. But the confidence we had both formerly felt in our own minds and in their powers had been shaken like a mouse by a cat.

"Socrates . . . I never expected . . . *that*."

"The unexpected must be a mark of the true God's presence," he retorted. "If you *had* expected it, it would not have been the true God. It would have been *your* God."

"I had hoped to ask a thousand questions about him. I was impatient with all those abstract philosophical questions you led me into before, not because I was impatient with questions but because I was impatient to get to the God-stuff, and to question *that*. But . . ." I groped for words.

"You had hoped to ask a thousand questions *about* him, and when you met him you had not a single question *to* him," Socrates noted. After a moment's thought, he added, "Exactly the same thing seems to have happened to Job."

"Do you think we will be allowed to go back to our old questioning mode of reason and logic?" I asked.

"Oh yes," he replied. "How else shall we choose between competing gods?"

"I thought there was only one," I objected.

"Indeed—in reality. But in our religions and our thoughts there are many. We still must choose, like a princess among rival suitors. Though we have gone beyond the land of philosophical questions and entered the land of religious ones, we have not left the life of questioning, or the spirit of philosophy as the love of wisdom."

"But isn't it impious somehow to subject God to human reason?"

"We will not do that. We will subject human religions to human reason. If one or more of them is from God, and not just from human invention, his wisdom will not be blown away by *our* little wind. But human follies may be."

"So we still have a long way to go and a lot of work to

do? The mountain was not the end?"

"It was the beginning," Socrates said.

"I had hoped that the mountain would be our end. We did . . . kind of . . . meet *God*, after all," I said, embarrassed at the sound of my own voice compared to the memory of his.

"Indeed. That is precisely why it is not our end but our beginning," Socrates replied.

"As you will find out when you die," he added, cryptically.

EIGHT

THE PANTHEIST
& THE DEIST

Is God
Everywhere or
Nowhere?

𝕫𝕦𝕫𝕦𝕫𝕦𝕫𝕦𝕫𝕦𝕫𝕦

*A*fter a while the path came to another fork, as I expected. However, this time there were—unexpectedly—
three roads, not two. The choice this time was not between
paths that led left and right horizontally, but among three
levels of height. The highest path led toward an arid, arctic
plain. The lowest road led down to a humid, swampy
jungle. The third led straight, then curved, so that one
could not see what lay beyond its turns. Two men, Greeks
in robes again, stood beckoning at this junction. They
mocked and contradicted each other's every word.

"What you seek is near! It is here! It is everywhere!" said
the man who stood at the fork that led to the swamp.

"What you seek is far! It is there! It is nowhere!" said the
other, who stood at the fork that led to the desert. He

added, "It is Without."

The swamp man immediately contradicted: "It is Within!"

The desert man cried: "It is beyond the All."

The swamp man retorted: "It *is* the All!"

Confused, I turned to Socrates for explanation. "Do you recognize these two?" I asked.

"I think so," he replied. "The man on the lower road seems to be Parmenides. You could call him the first philosophical pantheist. The man on the higher road seems to be Aristotle. You could call him the first philosophical deist."

"Do they agree about *anything?*" I asked.

"Why don't you ask them?" Socrates suggested.

I tried this opening: "Tell me, you who would be my guides: is the divine one or many?"

"One only," said Parmenides. "As the holy Hindu scriptures say, 'One' is the word of all wisdom, 'Two' is the beginning of all illusion."

I wondered whether Parmenides had learned from India during his lifetime in Greece or after death. But I did not let my historical curiosity distract me from my central task. "Then why are there so *many* growing things in your jungle?" I asked.

"Because the One is manifested in the many. So the masses worship many gods, while the mystics know the One. The masses see the many masks, while the mystic sees the One behind them."

"Then why not tell the masses the truth?" I asked naively. "You seem to teach two different truths, one for the masses and another for the mystics."

"True. Truth is manifold," he said.

"So Reality is one, yet Truth is many?" I asked (thinking

the question very Socratic).

"Yes."

"How can that be? What 'Truth' do you peddle that is the opposite of Reality? Who would want such an unreal 'Truth'?" I asked, suspicious of one who would not give the whole truth to the whole people.

"Away from this ignorant heathen!" cried Aristotle. "He drags down the divine to the level of human beings and even beasts. His people worship a thousand idols—uneducated fools!"

At these words my suspicion of elitism arose again, now directed to Aristotle. "What about your people?" I asked him.

"They are educated. They are sons of enlightenment. They keep God pure of nature and nature pure of God and free for Science." Here he bowed, as he verbally capitalized the *S*. (And here I thought he was about to transform into John Locke, or Immanuel Kant. But this may have been my imagination.) "Not mysticism but reason is my religion."

"And how many follow your religion, Aristotle? As many as follow his?"

"No, but quality is more important than quantity."

"So his God is for the many and yours is for the few?"

"For the enlightened."

"And what of the unenlightened?" I was now beginning to suspect that these two opposite religions were really quite similar in their "few-versus-many" elitism.

"They make God in their own image," Aristotle replied. "As even Xenophanes has said, if donkeys were theologians, God would be the Super-Donkey. Since the unenlightened are human, they see God as a Super-Man. That's because they don't follow reason."

"What do they follow instead?"

"Their heart. They want warmth, and love, and inti-macy—a God up close, like a lover. A God they can 'relate to.' "

"Well, I understand that. There is surely a big difference between a Mind Behind Nature and a God who loves you like a Father."

"Indeed there is," Aristotle admitted. "That's just the point. There's no *reason*, only *desire*, behind the idea that God loves you. Why should God love you if he is perfect and has no needs, no desires? Where did you ever get such a wild, crazy idea? It's like saying you love some bacteria. It's a category confusion, like saying Eternal Truth got thirsty."

"But that's what the many do think, isn't it?"

"Yes."

"Where do you think they got that idea?"

"Unthinking tradition and authority, of course."

"But where do you think the authorities got it in the first place? How did the tradition get started? And why has it become so popular?"

"I have no idea. It's just ridiculous. People are just stupid, that's all."

"Haven't you ever wondered, and investigated where they got it from?"

"Why waste my time?"

"Because there just might be something to it."

"How could it be?"

"Well, if it comes to that, why couldn't it?"

"Because it's such an arrogant idea! What gives you the right to think God loves *you?*"

"Well, if it comes to that, what gives you the right to claim you know God so well that you know he couldn't love you? Isn't that even more arrogant?"

"But what evidence is there for it? Does nature show you a loving God?—'Nature red in tooth and claw'?"

"No."

"History, then? The bloodbath, the worldwide butcher shop?"

"No."

"Then what?"

I could not answer his question—at least not yet, not until I had investigated the claim made by the many. And in light of the experience that had overwhelmed us on the mountain, I did not think it seemed very likely that such a high God would stoop so low. Yet I could not dismiss a thing believed by so many without ever having inquired into it, and I resolved to do so in the near future.

For the present, I had to investigate the claims of the two men in front of me. I thought I had discovered a second thing on which they agreed, in addition to their elitism. "God is not a Person, then?" I asked Aristotle.

"Of course not," he said.

"I don't mean a *human* person, with an animal body, of course," I explained.

"What other kind could there be?" he asked, genuinely surprised.

"Oh, I don't know. Many kinds, I suppose—angels, goddesses, ghosts, elves, extraterrestrials—who knows? How do you know?"

"No, no, that is a low, vulgar idea. God is a Substance, a Force, a Pure Act, not a Person."

"Is an impersonal Force higher than a Person? Is it higher to be something like electricity than to be something like Aristotle?"

"A Mind, then. A cosmic Mind. A Mind, not a man."

"Of course God is not a *man*," I said. "Do you really

think that's what the masses believe?"

"Oh, yes," he said.

"And how do you know this?"

"Why, everyone knows that. Everyone who's educated, that is. All the best books and teachers will tell you that."

"But the masses themselves—what do they tell you?"

"Why be instructed by them when we have pure reason instead?"

I was now quite convinced that Aristotle was as elitist as Parmenides, and that both agreed that whatever God was, he could not be a Person, as the masses thought. I thought I then detected a third agreement between them, and I tested this third thought as follows.

"Parmenides, do you say God is Within?"

"Yes," he said.

"And Aristotle, do you say God is Beyond?"

"Yes," he said.

"So you agree that God must be either Beyond or Within?"

"Of course," they said.

"Why could he not be both?" I asked.

Both philosophers were silent. Then, "How could that be?" they asked, in unison.

"I don't know," I answered. "But I certainly would like to find out. And whatever God turns out to be, I think he will escape the two opposite little boxes you have made for him. I think I will take the middle path—not because I know what surprises lurk around its corners, but precisely because I do *not* know. The real God is bound to surprise us—that at least I know. He is more like a storm, or like an animal, than like a concept: something real, not just something thought.

"And here, I think, is a fourth thing you have in common. Your God is more like a dream, or a diagram. I think God is more like a dog than like a dream or a diagram."

They were both scandalized at this thought. "Are you dyslexic?" asked Aristotle. "You have 'God' exactly backwards!"

"I didn't say God *was* a dog. I said he was more like a dog than a diagram—real, not mental; alive, not dead."

"So you would rather worship a dog than a diagram."

"I think I would."

"Well then," said Parmenides, "there are many sacred cows and monkeys down in my jungle, if that's the kind of thing you're into."

"No thank you," I said.

"You want to be more scientific than that, I hope," said Aristotle.

"Yes I do. I want to be very scientific. And the first rule of a scientific theory is that it must fit all the data. That's why I can't buy yours. You see, I've already met the data."

" 'Met'? How can this be?" they cried, again in unison. "How could a man meet God?"

That settled it for me. I turned to leave and called out to both, "Sorry about your God, but mine's got to be at least as real as a dog. And alive. Yours seems pretty dead."

As I stalked down the middle road, Socrates followed silently and thoughtfully behind me.

This was the first time he had been totally silent. I thought, *I did that all by myself,* and the thought made me feel proud. But the thought continued: *Perhaps I won't be needing him much longer*—and this made me feel very sad.

NINE

THE JEW

Could His-Story Be a Non-Prophet Organization?

𝔯𝔲𝔯𝔲𝔯𝔲𝔯𝔲𝔯𝔲

*A*s *we walked down the curving road, I explored the thought* of Socrates' increasing silence and my increasing speech. Ever since our encounter on the mountain, he had been uncharacteristically subdued. I asked him, "Socrates, have you lost your taste for argument? You've been letting me carry the ball lately. Is it because of what we saw and heard back there on the mount?"

"In one sense, yes, of course," he answered. "Only a fool would now prefer prattling to pondering. But in another sense, no. That encounter has stimulated my thought, not stultified it. It raises a host of new questions."

"But . . . but . . ." I could not quite formulate my question. "All this new stuff—faith, and religion, and relationship with God—isn't that miles away from reason and philosophy and logic?"

"Why do you think so?"

"Well, they seem exact opposites."

"How?"

"Isn't faith a kind of holding fast? And isn't questioning a kind of testing? And aren't those two opposites?"

Socrates replied, "Isn't there a piece of advice in your Bible that says: 'Test all things; hold fast to that which is good'?"

"I think that's right," I said, remembering some echoes from my youth and wondering whether Socrates read my mind or my Bible.

He continued, "So it puts these two things together. It tells you first to test all things, to question. *Then* to hold fast to what you've found to be good. But how do you know what's good until you test it? How can you select a faith except by questioning and reasoning?"

"That makes sense," I said. "Why then have you been silent?"

"For your sake, not mine. My task is nearly complete."

I looked at him despondently. "You are about to leave me?"

"I am here so that you may learn from me the most important lesson I can teach: how to learn by yourself. A good teacher makes himself increasingly dispensable."

The thought occurred to me that perhaps I would pretend to be a little stupider just to keep my beloved teacher around a little longer. But Socrates assured me, "Do not fear; you will not *want* me around much longer, I think. For you are about to meet another."

I wondered who this could be, and as if in immediate answer another fork appeared in our road, as it ended, like a *T*, and I had to turn left or right. To the left led a desert path that ran to the shore of a faraway sea, and to the right another desert path led to the bank of an equally faraway river. My eyes seemed to have acquired telescopic vision in this country, for both bodies of water were many, many miles distant.

I was immediately heartened by the sight of the sea, as most members of our species are, but even more intrigued by what I saw approaching on the road from the sea: an enormous crowd, variously dressed in sandals, loincloths, cloaks, robes, rags and turbans, composed of rich and poor, with many small and large children, animals and carts laden with possessions ranging from wicker and wattle to silver and gold. They were all following one man.

This man was old but large and strong, and he seemed to smell of water, as if he had been born in a river, or as if he had just come out of the sea, or both. I say "smell," but the smell was not detectable by the nose, but by the spirit. Around his neck, where some wear a locket with a picture of their home and family as a reminder of their origin, he wore a necklace of bulrushes. Both he and the people following him looked immensely tired and poor, but there was an iron resolution in his eyes and a light around his face that reminded me of the light that had surrounded both Socrates' body and my own on the mountaintop.

With my preternaturally sharp vision, I saw, as through a telescope, standing by the sea many miles to my left a very different crowd of people, to whom I was immediately attracted. These people were even more numerous than the desert wanderers. They were dressed in rich and beautiful blues and golds, their bodies were sleek and clean, their hair brushed and bejeweled, their stomachs round and full, and their stores well stocked with meat.

Whereas the desert wanderers were accompanied by dirty, scraggly goats and donkeys, the rich people over the sea were accompanied by many sleek and beautiful cats. But I saw no very young children among them.

My choice was evidently between these two people: either to join the motley crowd of wanderers or to seek the Beautiful People from whom they had apparently come. The choice seemed obvious: the rich or the poor, the many or the few, the rested or the weary, the fed or the hungry, the sea or the desert. But I had to investigate before I chose; that, at least, I had learned from Socrates. Especially this time, for this choice was evidently to be not merely the choice of an abstract, timeless philosophy but of a concrete people moving through time and history. Which group would I follow? Who would bring me to my quest's goal?

I turned to Socrates as the wanderers approached. "Socrates, I see what the Beautiful People have to offer me that you do not have. But I do not see what this man and his people could possibly have."

"It is not what he has, it is what he seeks," said Socrates, who evidently knew all about him and had guided me deliberately to just this point and this meeting.

"What does he seek?" I asked.

"The Promised Land!" thundered the big man, who had by now reached us. He did not stop or slacken his stride. We would have to hurry to walk with him if we wanted to converse with him; else he and his people would pass us by. Thus my first choice, though only temporary and revocable, was made: I chose not to ignore this man and let him pass.

"You are a strange-looking people," I began.

"Looks are not always deceiving," he answered. "We *are* a strange people. We are different from all others."

"What makes you different?"

"Many things, most of which you cannot see, at least not yet. But one thing you can see: we are not a people with a land, a people settled and secure. We are nomads, pilgrims, wanderers."

"Are you lost?"

"No," he said; but before he could continue, a clever-looking woman who was walking beside him piped up, "Tell the truth, Moses!" Then, turning to me, she said, "We sure *are* lost. And why? Because my macho man here is too proud to stop and ask directions!"

Moses blushed and tried to ignore her, as one to whom a dentist is unthinkable tries to ignore a toothache. But she kept muttering many words, of which I caught only *meshuggina*. I wished I could have heard her account of the journey as well as Moses'.

"We are not *wholly* lost," corrected Moses. "For we know whence we came and whither we are going. We came from Egypt, there"—he gestured down the road to the sea and the Beautiful People—"and we seek the Promised Land." Here he gazed longingly in the other direction.

"Why?" I asked.

"What do you mean, 'why?' " He seemed surprised by my question.

"Why do you seek the Promised Land? Why not stay with the Beautiful People?"

"Oh. Well, for one thing, life among them was anything but beautiful for *us*," he said. "We were their slaves. But the main reason is very simple. We seek the Promised Land because it has been promised to us."

"By whom?"

"By God. We are God's chosen people."

"You speak to God?"

"God speaks to us, and will speak through us to the whole world."

"That's quite a claim!" I said, thinking this sounded even more arrogant than the deism of Xenophanes and the pantheism of Parmenides.

"It's not a claim for us, but for God," explained Moses. "Whatever our achievements, they're God's doing, not ours. Our claim to be God's chosen people is the humblest interpretation possible to put on the data of our miraculous survival."

"Your claim is going to scandalize a lot of people," I observed.

"I know," said Moses. "We are like a lump of lead in the stomach—undigested, unassimilated."

I reflected that the later name for this people was one of the few words that still had bite and sting and power even in an age of weak, weary and dissipated words. The word *Jew* was a sacrament of the difference between the concrete and the abstract, the particular and the universal; it incarnated "the scandal of particularity." An unassimilated name for an unassimilated people.

"Look here," I said, a little short of breath for having to speak as I walked briskly to keep up with Moses, "I wish you people well, and I am certainly not anti-Semitic. But I am not a Jew either. I don't belong here."

"Why not?"

"Why not? What a silly question! Because I am of a different race."

"Oh, you are a racist, then?"

"Certainly not!"

"But if it is race that determines your philosophy and your identity, you are a racist. If race is the most important thing to you, you are a racist. If you will not share our quest and our faith simply because you are not of our race, you are a racist."

My first thought, upon being thus accused, was to wonder where Socrates was. I looked behind me to seek his help in defending myself against this surprisingly Socratic argument from Moses. But Socrates was trudging down the road away from us, probably looking for another student to guide.

I was on my own now, and I had to exemplify Socrates' utter honesty whether or not I could exemplify his logical skill. So I said, "You are right, Moses. I cannot let my race choose my convictions or my faith or my hope. So tell me, why should I embrace yours and your people's? Give me reasons."

"Because we are God's prophet."

"Prophets, you mean?"

"Prophet. Singular. Or rather, collective. God's collective prophet to the world. His mouthpiece. It sounds elitist, I know, but we are 'chosen' not to bask in privilege but to serve and to suffer."

"To serve—how?"

"By teaching, for one thing."

"Teaching what to whom?"

"Teaching God to the world. That's what prophets do. The word means 'mouthpiece.' "

"Tell me the first thing you teach about God."

"That he created the universe."

"As an artist creates a work of art?"

"Something like that. But he created out of nothing."

"And you can know something of the artist, or the creator, from looking at his art, or his creation, is that right?"

"Yes indeed."

"So we can know much about God from nature?"

"Indeed we can. His existence and his power and his intelligence are revealed there."

"Then why do we need prophets?"

Moses' answer surprised me. "Because of sin," he said.

"Sin?"

"Sin. Rebellion against God, and his will, and his law. Sin blinds the mind. Sin makes us forget God, and his will, and his law. It makes us rationalize instead of reasoning. So God sends prophets to remind us."

"So you are God's big mouth to the world?"

"We are that."

"And you?"

"I am his mouth to his mouth."

The claim challenged me, but I had to look before I leaped. I demanded, "Tell me why I should believe this. I will not choose without good reasons. I am a disciple of Socrates; I will not make a leap in the dark."

"No one but a fool does that," replied Moses. "I will give you good reasons. But they will not be abstract reasons, like those Socrates gave you." (Again I wondered: *How does he know?* But again I resisted the temptation to diversion.) "I will give you concrete reasons. Historical reasons, since our claim is a concrete and historical claim," he said.

"Are there proofs?" I demanded to know.

"Historical reasons are not proofs. They are stronger than proofs, and also weaker. Weaker because they leave you room to doubt, and to choose. Stronger because they are not abstract arguments but concrete *clues* in history, like footprints in desert sands."

"Clues to the Jews, eh? What are they?"

"Our very existence, for one thing. Our survival. Everybody wants to wipe us out. And nobody can. We hold together. We are all brothers, entirely descended from one man, Abraham—a single family. This people is the oldest in the world, especially by the time you come on the scene. We last, while Greece and Rome and America perish."

"OK, that's a concrete clue. What else?"

"The miracles God did for us, for another thing. Some of them are recorded in the Bible."

"Of course if the Bible lies, then maybe there were no miracles."

"But that's a third miracle: the Bible. The world's most influential book. And one of the oldest. More people have read it than any other book. More people trust it than any other book. To say it's a pack of lies, you have to be an elitist and say that most people are deeply deceived."

"Hmm. What else?"

"Our law."

"You mean the Ten Commandments."

"Yes, and also the rest of the Torah. It's the world's most perfect law, and the oldest that survives. And it's the only one that has been continually observed by any people. Read Josephus or Philo sometime."

"Where did you get this law?"

"On Mount Sinai back there." Here Moses pointed to the very mountain Socrates and I had climbed. "From God. They're God's idea, not mine."

I could believe that now. He continued, "And this law is not an easy one to observe. It is pure and perfect and high and holy and demanding and severe and rigorous. It is truly a miracle that the law has been preserved and lived by a people as rebellious as this one—and without a homeland for much of its history too. All other peoples have changed their laws, even though they were less demanding than ours."

"That's clue number four. Any more?"

"Our honesty. Faithfully we preserve the law and the prophets, even though the prophets condemn us and insult us and constantly call us to task in God's name. We don't change a jot or a tittle. God's got this thing about jots and tittles."

"That's impressive. That's five clues. Any more?"

"Secular clues as well as religious ones. Clues of reason and intelligence as well as faith and morality. Our secular achievements have already been remarkable, and will be even more remarkable in the future. We are tough, and smart, and strong-willed and practical (and also theoretical). We are achievers. We outcreate and outdiscover people a thousand times our size. We supply a ridiculously disproportionate number of the world's scientists and philosophers and lawyers and scholars."

"Enough, already. Not proofs, but impressive clues, I admit."

"But you haven't heard our chief claim to fame yet."

"What's that?"

"We know God as nobody else does. Compare our idea of God to any other one, and it's like comparing a star with a mud puddle. Now that's either our achievement or his. If it's ours, we're superior. If it's his, we're only his prophets, his mouth."

"Tell me about this unique idea of God."

"For one thing, nearly everybody else around us thinks there are many, but we know there's only one of him."

"Oh, I know that already."

"Sure you do. But do you know why? Because of us. Once we were the only people in the world who knew that."

"OK, what else?"

"That he's infinitely perfect. No flaws. No sins, no self-ishness, no injustice, no changing his mind, no being bribed. He's holy—unlike all the other peoples' gods."

"OK, that's number two. What else?"

"That he created the universe."

"But all cultures have creation myths."

"No they don't. They have *formation* myths."

"What's the difference?"

"Our God gave the universe not just its shape or its motion but its very existence. He created it out of nothing, not out of something. Matter itself is his creation, not just form. It's a unique idea. The Greek philosophers called us crazy for believing it."

"OK, that's three."

"And that therefore he is omnipotent, unlimited in power, able to work miracles simply by willing them. He thought the universe into existence, so he can do the same with anything else. After banging out the Big Bang, he can add any little bangs he wants."

"OK, that's four."

"And that he is all-wise, all-knowing. Never makes a mistake. You can't ever fool him, as you can fool the pagans' gods sometimes."

"That's five."

"And he has a will as well as a mind. He wills the good. His will is the source of the moral law."

"Well, of course. What other kind of God would you want to believe in except a good one, a moral one?"

"The answer the Gentile world has given is: almost any other kind imaginable. Again you mistake our gift for your own discovery! We're the only people who joined and explained two of the deepest instincts in human nature: the instinct to worship and the instinct of

conscience. The God we worship is the God we're morally obligated to, the one who commands us, both through
the law on these stone tablets"—here he gestured toward
a box on poles carried by four men—"and through the law
he put in our hearts."

"OK, that's six."

"And that he loves us."

I pulled up short at this. I remembered—and echoed—
the shock this idea had produced in Parmenides and Aristotle. "Why would he do that?" I demanded. "If he's
perfect, he's not lonely or incomplete in any way. So he has
no needs, and therefore no need for us."

"True. His love is pure gift-love, not need-love. You see,
that also explains creation. If he's perfect, he had no need
at all for any creature. So the only possible motive for his
creating creatures was love."

"But they weren't there to love before he created them."

"Exactly. He loved them into existence. You see, his love
isn't a response to something lovable that's already there.
His love creates that something, creates its own object, and
makes it lovable."

"That's an incredible notion, the notion of this more-
than-perfect God of yours. How did you ever find it?"

"It's not a *notion*, it's a reality. And we didn't find him;
he found us."

"I think I know what you mean," I said, remembering
the mountain. "But what would you say to those who have
never felt confronted by anything like God? Is there some
argument, or some experiment, or some meditation exer-
cise or some set of good works that we can do that would
bring him into our experience?"

"No."

"Is that it? Just 'no'?"

"He is not a pagan god who can be manipulated by priests or philosophers."

"So there's nothing we can do, then? It's blind faith? There's no experiment, no data, nothing scientific?"

"Sure there is. There's data."

"What data?"

"Us. Jews. This people. Our history, our prophets, our law, our scriptures, our miracles. That's your data, your divine footprint in history's sands. Come with us and you'll see. Come and see."

"I don't know . . ."

"Of course you don't. Not before you *look*. That's why you have to come and see: not because you know but because you don't know. What could be more scientific and more Socratic than that? Come and see for yourself."

"It's an investment, a risk . . ."

"Of course it is. Everything really worthwhile is. Life, love, liberty. How could this not be the same?"

"Moses, I will come with you," I said, with sudden decisiveness. "I may regret it, but if I do, at least I'll know. If I don't come with you, I'll never know, and maybe will always regret it. I just *have* to know. So I'll come and see. Say, Moses, where did you learn such good philosophy? I never thought you'd convince me."

"Oh, I met Socrates long before you did. You see, I died about thirty-five centuries before you were born." Moses dropped the remark casually, but when I heard it I stopped in my tracks (all during this conversation neither of us had broken stride), and then I had to run to catch up with him.

When I did, I realized that Socrates had *not* abandoned me. I now had two Socrateses, or rather two better-than-Socrateses, one within and one without.

TEN

THE MESSIAH

Is Jesus Lord, Liar or Lunatic?

𝕫𝕣𝕫𝕣𝕫𝕣𝕫𝕣𝕣

*M*oses and his motley crew marched on toward their Promised Land, and I marched with them, seeking *my* Promised Land of the Truth. Time passed differently in this world: I do not recall eating or sleeping or being either hungry or tired, though we must have marched hundreds of miles in every possible geometrical configuration, sometimes even straight.

Many times during this long and dusty journey I doubted the wisdom of my choice to cast my lot with these people by letting them be my new, post-Socratic guides and teachers. But their strong faith and sense of destiny impressed me, and the God they said had revealed himself to them and would reveal himself through them to the world—the absolutely Perfect One—this God seemed the only God worthy of occupying the throne room in my heart and in my life, if only I deeply "knew myself," as Socrates would have it, and deeply respected myself, as my more modern psychologists would put it.

Every time I was tempted to look back and wonder whether I would not have been happier with the Beautiful People, the same answer came to my doubts: the comparison between these ragtag wandering poor and those sleek and established rich was corrected by the comparison between their perfect God and the obviously imperfect gods of the Beautiful People, whether these gods were ghosts or cats or demons or dollars. The Jews were the truly rich people, the spiritually rich; the pagans were the spiritually poor.

I was learning to see with deeper eyes. When I turned to see the Beautiful People now, I saw an enormous pyramid hovering over the whole immense mass of those milling millions, enclosing them in its copious underground tunnels, preparing them for burial. The pyramid was faceless, and when I looked at the people inside it, *they* were faceless too. Each was only a skeleton and a skull.

The following thought occurred to me: Since I had apparently moved on from the idea-market of philosophy to that of religion, and since a God demanded not only one's mind but one's life, I had better be sure not to give my life to some faceless, dead thing, or to a Lord of Death, but to the living God, the Lord of Life and the Stronger-Than-Death. In this connection I was moved by the thing Moses kept preaching to his people as the command of their God: "Choose life."

Those two words became Moses' last. Before the road reached the river, he disappeared into the sky, it seemed, after climbing another mountain. Somehow I knew that his bones, unlike those of the Egyptians, would never be found in any tomb.

Soon after Moses' departure, the road reached the river, and I knew I was about to confront another fundamental choice of ways.

The man who had replaced Moses as the leader of this people was named Joshua, or Jesus. As Moses had crossed the sea, Joshua crossed the river, which parted before him. Some of the people followed him, as I did, and some stayed behind.

Then a strange thing happened. My journey became even more like a vision. The road led up a hill far away, where stood three old rugged crosses. The middle one had a sign that read "This is the King of the Jews." Joshua mounted the middle cross, looked at me from this bloody throne and invited me to come closer.

Naturally, I hesitated, looking for a more attractive alternative. I turned around to see what seemed to be a mirror image of the hill and the three crosses, each with a sign on top as Joshua's cross had had. The first sign read "Great is Diana of the Ephesians." As I gazed, the cross under this sign turned into a bed, and I saw millions of men, like mice, trying to mate with an enormous, scantily clad woman whose lips dripped scarlet blood. As I looked, she metamorphosed into a dragon.

The second sign, on the second cross, read "Moloch"; and as I looked, the cross under it turned into a golden brazier shaped like a gaping maw. I saw mothers and fathers standing in a long, long line, waiting to deliver their babies to the priests standing by the brazier, who then tore out the babies' hearts with a stone knife, threw the still-beating hearts into the grinning mouth of the brazier and tossed the other body parts to a large dog (which they named "Dumpster").

The sign on the third cross read "Pan." This cross too quickly changed shape to become a set of pipes held by a dancing man who was a goat from the navel down. His face was first Jim Morrison, then Mick Jagger. He danced a strange, writhing dance around his own genitalia as if they were the still point of the turning world, and he paused frequently to bow in profound self-adoration.

As I turned back from this unholy trinity, Joshua's cross also changed shape. It became a crown. Its jewels were diamonds in the shape of sharp thorns.

I was now wondering whether reason had simply been left behind in this flood of images, and how I was to make up my mind and choose my way. As soon as my mind formulated this question, I saw a ruddy, round-faced Irishman who looked more like a farmer than a philosopher, separating himself from the crowd that was now milling beneath the crosses. "Hullo!" he boomed. "I have come to help you choose your next step."

"Who are you?" I asked.

"My name is C. S. Lewis, but you can call me Jack."

I was disappointed that my substitute for Moses was *less* than Moses, whereas Moses had been *more* than Socrates. But I remembered the saying of John the Baptist, who had had the same function of helping people to find the Messiah: "He must increase, and I must decrease."

"What are you doing here?" I demanded. I knew the name of Lewis, having read a few of his crystal-clear books and seen the movie *Shadowlands*.

"The same thing I did on earth. The same thing Socrates and John the Baptist did: pointing to the truth. As Socrates said, philosophers have job security even after death."

"So you're here to give me reasons for believing that this Jesus-Joshua is Moses' successor as my prophet and Socrates' successor as my teacher?"

"Much more than that. His claim on you is to be more than your teacher, like Socrates, and more than your prophet, like Moses. His claim is to be your God."

"What! That's impossible. He's a man. God is not a man."

"With God all things are possible. Therefore it is possible for God to become a man."

"But . . . it staggers belief."

"Indeed. Congratulations for seeing that, at least. Many don't."

"Do you really mean you believe, and you want me to believe, that *that man*, that man who's hanging there dying, that man who came from a woman's womb and was a baby who couldn't talk, that man who got hungry, and got splinters, and got constipated—*that* is *God*? I think I have never heard anything more ridiculous in all my life."

"You have never heard anything more amazing, but you have heard many things more ridiculous. One of them is that God could never do that, that God would only do the reasonable and expected things that *you* would do if *you* were God."

"I still don't see how God could do that."

"Why couldn't he? Couldn't an author put himself into his own novel as one of his characters?"

"I suppose so."

"And if he did, he would then be exactly what you decided to look for awhile ago in your encounter with the deist Aristotle and the pantheist Parmenides: a God who was totally transcendent and totally immanent at the same time. The author is both transcendent to his story, as its creator, and immanent in it, as a creature. If even a human author can do this, why can't God?"

I had no answer. "But—even if that is *possible*, why should I believe it really happened?"

"Because he said so."

"Sheer authority?"

"*His* authority. *He* claimed this. That's where Christians got the idea: from him."

"How do I know his disciples didn't make it up?"

"Because all the first Christians were Jews, and that's the last thing a Jew would make up. Pagans might divinize their human heroes, because their gods were very much like humans to begin with. But to Jews it would have been just what it is to you now: unthinkable, the supreme foolishness, because their God is so absolutely transcendent and perfect. And it was also to them the supreme blasphemy, worthy of death—of crucifixion."

"So his followers couldn't have made up this whole thing about his being God because they were good Jews?"

"Yes."

"All right then, why couldn't they be bad Jews? Liars? Blasphemers? Just because people *claim* some strange story is true, that doesn't prove it's true. The storyteller may be lying."

"But they all died for their belief in this story. Eleven of his twelve apostles were martyred for not giving up this new faith of theirs. And thousands of their followers did the same. Nothing proves sincerity like martyrdom."

"OK, so they believed it. That doesn't prove it's true."

"But what could have led them to believe such a shocking idea? Remember, they weren't pagans, they were Jews. How could a Jew have confused God with a man? That never happened once, ever, either before or since, in four thousand years of Jewish history."

"Oh," I said.

"And the same applies even more forcefully to Jesus himself. Is he such a lunatic that he thinks he's God? Or is he a liar? If he's not God, as he claimed to be, he's either a liar or a lunatic. Can you call this man a lunatic?—the man even non-Christians acknowledge as one of the wisest men of all time? Or will you call this man a deliberate liar—the man even all non-Christians acknowledge to be a saint?"

"It does seem shocking. But it also seems shocking to call a man God. Let's go over the possibilities again."

"An excellent idea. First, the liar possibility . . ."

"Yes. Why is that not just unlikely but impossible?"

"Why do liars lie?"

"Many reasons."

"What's common to all of them?"

"I don't know, I guess the liar thinks he's going to get *something* out of his lie, but it could be many different things."

"Exactly. Liars lie to get something for themselves. Now what did Jesus get out of his lie? Hated, misunderstood, rejected, betrayed, persecuted, spit on, whipped, tried, tortured and crucified. Hardly a list of perks! And his disciples got the very same things out of it, if *they* are the ones who invented the lie."

"That makes no sense at all. OK, let's try 'lunatic' again. Why couldn't he be a lunatic?"

"Too smart. Too wise. Too canny. Too good with people. Above all, too *interesting*. Lunatics are really very dull once you get to know them. They're in a rut. They're just the opposite of creative. Lunatics have *less* wisdom and creativity and love than ordinary people; he has *more*. If he's the definition of lunacy, then a world of lunatics would be heaven on earth. If he's what a lunatic looks like, we should envy them, not pity them or try to cure them."

"Of course. But the only alternative left—that he's God—seems equally impossible."

"Startling, yes, but not *impossible*. Look at the hypothesis. If he's *God*, why couldn't he do anything? God is all-powerful. 'With God all things are possible.' If God could create the entire universe out of nothing, why couldn't he incarnate himself in one person within that universe? Who are you to tell God what he can and can't do, anyway?"

"That's putting it bluntly, but I get your point."

"And there are a lot of positive clues, divine fingerprints, so to speak. The miracles, especially rising from the dead. Is that within human power?"

"Obviously not," I admitted.

"It even seems to be in the divine *style*," he added. "The God of the Jews, the God of Moses, is the God of life, not of death. So it would be very much up his alley to conquer death."

I was impressed with this stylistic twist Lewis put on the argument. The fingerprints certainly seemed to fit. But I wanted more certainty.

"If I saw him rise from the dead, I'd probably believe in him too," I said. "But I didn't see it. I have only your word for it, or the church's word for it, or the Bible's word for it. I don't like to argue from authority."

"I'm not arguing from authority," Lewis replied, "And if I were, it certainly wouldn't be *my* authority. Just look at it logically. If he didn't rise from the dead—the clearest proof that he's more than a man—then his apostles and their successors, who told the world that he did, didn't tell the truth. Right so far?"

"Of course."

"Now if you tell an untruth, either you know it's untrue or you don't. If you know it's untrue, you're a liar, a deceiver. If you don't know it's untrue, you're deceived yourself. Right so far?"

"Yes, those are the only two possibilities. They were either deceivers or deceived."

"So let's try those two possibilities."

"All right. Why couldn't they be the liars? They weren't as wise and good as Jesus."

"Because they were martyrs. Nothing proves sincerity more than martyrdom, remember? If it was a lie, why did they die for it? Why did they never crack under torture? Why did not one Christian ever let the cat out of the bag and reveal that it was all a lie they had made up? Because that cat never was in that bag."

"Hmm . . . OK, so they were sincere and not liars. Why couldn't they be hallucinating? Sincerely deceived? A bit stupid and naive and credulous, ready to believe almost anything?"

"How stupid do you think you have to be to confuse a corpse with a living man?"

"Well . . . suppose it was all sort of vague and misty and uncertain?"

"Look at your data. It was just the opposite. Their claim, in all four Gospels, was very specific, very empirical. They *saw* him with their eyes, not in a vision. They talked with him, and he talked back. They touched him. 'Doubting Thomas' touched his wounds. They watched him eat food on two occasions after the resurrection. He stayed with them for forty days. Does that sound like a hallucination, or a vision, or a vague confusion?"

"But people do get very confused sometimes and hallucinate very weirdly and wildly."

"Sure they do. But hallucinations are private experiences. Very rarely do two or more people have the same hallucination. And when they do, it's never that concrete. And it never stays around for forty days. Or is seen by five hundred people."

"Five hundred?"

"That's what Paul says in First Corinthians. He says that most of these five hundred are still alive, thus inviting his readers to interview them, to check out the data for themselves. Does that sound like a vague and misty hallucination? Show me another hallucination in all of human history that behaved like that."

"But that's only what's written on paper. That's only the story in the Bible. That's not hard data. You weren't there to see it. You have to just believe it. It's an argument from authority."

"No it isn't. There *is* hard data: the New Testament texts. They refute the hallucination hypothesis. Even if it is a lie, it's not a lie about a hallucination, it's a lie about a resurrection. Let's get the story straight at least; let's not change the data."

"All right, but maybe it's only a *story* about a resurrection instead of a real resurrection."

"Then it's a lie. Then we're back to our first possibility."

"But . . . but . . ."

"But what?"

"I don't know. You're just backing me into a corner."

"Not I, but Reason does that. Haven't you learned as much from Socrates? Follow the argument wherever it leads. It's not I but reality that backs you into that corner."

"Well, I don't like it."

"Why not? Ask yourself what's going on in yourself

now. Reason and faith, reason and religion, now appear to be allies against something else that's holding you back from both. It's not reason holding you back from faith, or faith holding you back from reason, but some irrational fear or passion holding you back from the faith that reason has led you to. And I think you know that's true."

I could not help being totally honest. "It's true!" I admitted.

"So if reason leads you to Christ, what holds you back?"

"His cross!" I blurted out. "The bloody mess, the splinters—I don't want to be up there with him. I want to go back to the Beautiful People. I want a little comfort and security. I want to control my own life. Whose life is it, anyway?"

"That's precisely the question," Lewis answered. "If he's your creator, it's his."

"And this terrible truth is what you people call a Gospel, a 'Good News'?"

"Yes, if you look at the whole of it. Don't you see why it's *good* to throw yourself into his arms? Why do converts and saints do it? What motivates them, besides reason?"

"It must be fear."

"No. It's love. Fear doesn't embrace martyrdom. Only love does. Just look at the story—the whole story. It's the most incredible love story ever told. A story of your creator becoming your lover, your soul's husband."

"Do you mean all souls are feminine to him? Men and women alike?"

"Yes. But he is more than a man. This is not just Romeo, this is God! The all-powerful, all-perfect, infinite, eternal God, who needs nothing at all, freely chose to love you so much that he became a mortal man and got tortured and killed on a cross out of love for you. If there's any reason not to believe that story, it's not because it sounds too terrible but because it sounds too wonderful, it sounds too good to be true. It's wilder than any fairy tale."

"Then why is it so hard to make the choice, the leap into his arms?"

"Because he demands everything. A blank check. Not just one day a week, or one tenth of your money, or five prayers a day. This is not like your earlier choices. This is not a choice between philosophies, this is a choice between gods."

"*Between* gods? You mean the other three crosses are the alternatives?"

"Yes. It's Christ or Diana, Christ or Moloch, Christ or Pan. The God of heaven or the God of this world. The true God or an idol. 'Choose ye this day whom ye will serve.' "

I remembered these words. They were Joshua's. Then I recognized the continuity between this man's Christian faith and Moses' and Joshua's Jewish faith, and the continuity between the God I had met on Mount Sinai and the God who hung on the cross. Both demanded All. And both deserved my All. "I know what you say is true," I admitted. (The very air in this country made self-deception impossible.) "But I think I am a coward. I think I cannot leap the abyss between me and him."

"You're right. You are, and you can't. But God can. He can do it in you. The leap is faith, and faith is a gift of God. You can't just conjure it up in yourself, by pressing some inner button. But God will give you that gift, if you really want it, if you ask him. Why don't you do that right now? Are you afraid he won't answer that prayer? Or are you afraid he *will?*"

"You hit the nail on the head," I admitted. "Perhaps I don't *want* to leap that fearful abyss in front of me."

"But there is an even more fearful abyss behind you, if you go back now."

"You mean the three false gods?"

"That, yes, and also your own honesty. If you go back now, you will know that you have rejected him. You cannot just stay where you are and neither accept him nor reject him. Whatever happens from now on, those days are over. You have been led out into the battlefield; you can no longer be a neutral observer. You must be either for him or against him.

"You have dared to seek the truth, from the very first choice you made back at the beginning of your path. Well, this is the point that fateful choice has brought you to. You have sought Truth? Well, you have found him. Your only two options are *yes* and *no*. There is no third. Evasions have all been exposed. This moment is like the moment of death: standing in the Light, exposed, defenseless, naked. You must now choose either to consummate your whole journey or to abort it."

I saw that Lewis spoke the truth. I also saw that I could not go back. My destiny led me on inexorably—and therefore I made the freest *and* most necessary choice in my life.

I looked into the face on the cross, who was still patiently inviting me into an adventure that had no limit, no guarantee and no strings attached, an adventure that simply demanded my all, my *me*.

I could not bargain with him. He was not a pussycat, he was Christ the Tiger. Many theologians may have tried to pull his claws, but I would not and could not. I had no rights over against him, as I did over against other human beings: he was the creator of my very being. How could Hamlet have rights over against Shakespeare?

Where would he lead me? What would he ask of me?

He might ask me to sacrifice for him not only my sins but my legitimate worldly goods and ambitions as well. And then again, he might not. He might ask me to sacrifice the understanding and respect of my friends or even my family. Or then again, he might not. He would almost certainly demand that I give up my demand for comfort and control and security. I had to loosen my grasp of the wheel of my ship and let him be captain. Why should I do that?

Then the simple answer struck me: if he is the Absolute, well then, he is the Absolute, and not comfort, or family, or friends, or control, or security, or even biological life itself. If he should require me to gouge out my left eye or to cut off my left arm for his sake and the sake of his kingdom and his heaven, it would be infinitely worth it. No price was too high to pay for eternity.

"Yes," I said.

And I was born.

Epilogue

Looking back on my whole journey, I now saw that I had made ten right turns—right as opposed to wrong, but also right as opposed to left—literally, but not in the political sense, since these were not political choices. Turning continually right, my path had been a spiral.

However, it did not spiral *in*, like a whirlpool or a boa constrictor, but *out*. I had been freed from the tiny confines of my cave of ego and its correlative world of what pleased and displeased this ego. I was now outdoors, with the winds of heaven blowing in my hair. I was breathing other airs, living in other categories: not pleasure versus pain, or even correct versus incorrect, but faith versus sin, love versus betrayal, hope versus despair, yes versus no to God.

Socrates had led me through my exodus from the cave;

Moses had led me through my exodus from slavery to the Promised Land; and now Lewis had led me to my final exodus, my final freedom. Only when I said yes to the terrible and wonderful invitation to give up *everything* to the God on the cross who had given up everything for me, only when I no longer tightly and fearfully grasped that precious life of which he was the Lord, but gave it up to him, was I was truly free.